NGOs : Management and Governance

NGOs : Management and Governance

B. D. Ram

Mahaveer & Sons
(Publishers & Distributors)
New Delhi-110002

NGOs: Management and Governance

First Published 2011

ISBN 978-81-8377-304-1

Published by :

MAHAVEER & SONS

(Publishers & Distributors)

H-2/16, Ansári Road, Darya Ganj,

(Near Shiv Mandir) New Delhi-110002

E-mail : mahaveersonspub@rediffmail.com

Ph. 011 23242069, Mob. 09899608339

PRINTED IN INDIA

Published by Mahaveer & Sons, Publishers & Distributors, H-2/16 Ansari Road, Near Shiv Mandir, Daryaganj, New Delhi-110002, Printed at Himanshu Printers, Delhi.

Contents

Preface

Non-governmental organization (NGO) is a term that has become widely accepted as referring to a legally constituted, non-governmental organization created by natural or legal persons with no participation or representation of any government. In the cases in which NGOs are funded totally or partially by governments, the NGO maintains its non-governmental status and excludes government representatives from membership in the organization. Unlike the term *intergovernmental organization*, "non-governmental organization" is a term in general use but is not a legal definition. In many jurisdictions these types of organization are defined as "civil society organizations" or referred to by other names. The number of internationally operating NGOs is estimated at 40,000. National numbers are even higher: Russia has 277,000 NGOs. India is estimated to have between 1 million and 2 million NGOs.

The most difficult question about the independence of NGOs is whether they come under governmental influence. Individual governments do at times try to influence the NGO community in a particular field, by establishing NGOs that promote their policies. This has been recognized by quite common use of the acronym GONGO, to label a government-organized NGO. Also, in more authoritarian societies, NGOs may find it very difficult to act independently and they may not receive acknowledgment from other political actors even when they are acting independently. Beyond these unusual situations, there is a widespread prejudice that government funding leads to government control. In the field of human rights, it would damage an NGO for such a perception to arise, so Amnesty International has strict rules that it will not accept direct government funding for normal activities. On the other hand, development and humanitarian relief NGOs need substantial resources, to run their operational programs, so most of them readily accept official funds. While these NGOs would like the security of a guaranteed budget for their administrative overheads, governments generally only want to support field costs for projects.

Nominally NGOs may appear to be independent, when they design their own programs, but government influence can arise indirectly if the program is designed to make it more likely that government grants or contracts will be forthcoming. On the other hand, confident experienced NGOs can appeal for funding for new approaches and in so doing cause government officials to re-assess policy. The best example of this is the way in which NGOs, particularly the International Planned Parenthood Federation, dragged governments into adopting population programs. There is no obvious method to identify the direction of influence, without detailed knowledge of the relationship between an NGO and a government. Environmental NGOs may have either type of funding relationship. Conservation and research groups may happily obtain government funds to support their programs: some are innovative and some are not. Beyond these situations, radical campaigning groups may be unwilling and unable to attract government funds.

This book reliable one stop reference on all issues pertaining to NGOs: management and Governance.

—Editor

1

Promoting Good Governance in the Management of NGOs

Good governance means the effective management of an NGO's resources in a manner that is open, transparent, accountable, equitable and responsive to people's needs. The rule of law, transparency, accountability and effectiveness of NGO management are all essential components of good governance.

This issue of governance is now widely regarded as one of the key ingredients for poverty alleviation and sustainable development which NGOs must not loose sight. There are vital leakage between good governance and sustainable developments. Since most NGOs, are aimed at becoming sustainable then good governance becomes a vital aspect of NGOs existence. Participatory approach or management is essential to the achievement of sustainable development because it helps to ensure good accountability and effectiveness. NGOs in developing countries often lack institutional capacities and resources. Funds from donors are poorly managed. To ensure effective and proper management of resources, good governance becomes an important aspect of every NGO. NGOs need to be accountable for their actions and performance. Without such accountability, NGOs face no pressure to meet reasonable standards of governance and to ensure that an acceptable standard of human, financial and material management is maintained.

The achievement of accountability, participation and effective institutions is not easy. They require a considerable range of technical expertise, skill and commitment of resources. We can now look at how good governance can be promoted in NGOs.

ACCOUNTABILITY OF NGOS

Ensuring the accountability of NGOs involves first of all creating the conditions which will allow for open expression of views, free dissemination of information and the rule of law which is essential to the effective functioning of every NGO NGOs in both the North and the South are being challenged and address issues concerning their accountability and representatives. The key question being asked are:

To whom are NGOs accountable?

Who or what do they represent?

The debate around these questions has grown as NGOs have come to extend the scope, breadth and depth of their work, and as their structures have come to include both private and participatory forms of control and various forms of incorporated or unincorporated entities.

The questions appear at first sight to have answer. An incorporated private NGO is controlled by and thus accountable to a Board of Management or trustees. These people derive no financial gain from the Organisation, and thus are independent in the sense that they do not have the vested interests even staff or those served by the NGO may have. In the participatory and thus also accountable to be its members.

More broadly, NGOs are accountable to the wider public through processes of registration and regulation. They will also be accountable to-funders through agreed reporting arrangements.

NGOs working with marginalised and disadvantaged people see themselves as representing the interests of such people. Those NGOs which are more involved in a particular aspect of disadvantage or with an issue of affecting the well-being of society as a whole see themselves as representing a cause of some kind rather than a specified group of people. In both cases the representation will be stronger where the NGO has a participatory rather than a private structure. But issues of the accountability and representatives of NGOs are more complex than the above might suggest.

The fact that it is not that simple is implicit in particular aspects of the above discussion. The private NGOS, can thus in reality be accountable to nobody but themselves. Private NGOs can also be used by individuals to pursue their egotistical or political ambitions under the guise of representing people or causes. Organizations which claim to be participatory organisations can, when closely scrutinized, turn out to have a narrow, disenfranchised or "token" base of membership, and thus in reality be privately controlled or even used for fraudulent purposes.

Just as the existence of a small number of fraudulent NGOs can bring the financial integrity and honesty of the great majority of NGOs into needless doubt, so too do the small number of NGOs that are unaccountable and unrepresentative attract unwarranted doubt and criticism to the majority. Most NGOs are controlled by people acting out of genuine personal concern and commitment, and operating with standards of honesty and integrity.

There are a number of ways in which NGOs can improve the quality of their governance and operations, and these are outlined in the following sections. Many NGOs already recognise the need for such improvements. Signs of them being made are abundant, as are debates about issues raised by the changes, and the following sections try to reflect them.

Improving NGO Governance and Operations

NGOs are improving both their governance and operations in the following ways: Stating their mission, values and objectives clearly and ensuring that their strategies and operations are at all times within them; Better management processes as well as financial management, accounting and budgeting, systems; Better human resource development and training within the organisation-of managers, administrators, project staff, board members, beneficiaries, members and volunteers; Better procedures to ensure that men and women have equal opportunities to participate effectively at all levels of the organisation, from members to leaders; Better means by which both the organisation, and its projects, services and activities are monitored, evaluated, and reviewed. Better information provision by and about NGOs. Better networking and alliance-building among NGOs.

Management

Work in NGOs has always been demanding. It has

traditionally attracted people having high ideals, boundless energy, creativity, commitment and resilience. It is a sector which has a high level of female participation among volunteers and staff as well as at a leadership level. Indeed, in some countries, such as Jamaica. The majority of NGO leaders are women. The explosion of NGO activities over the recent past has not only been quantitative, but quantitative, too. As has been noted, NGOs can now be very large and complex entities, financing and running their own programmes as well as being contracted by government and others to be providers and deliverers of public services. They may simultaneously operate a number of activities, from service delivery to advocacy and campaigning. At the same time they will be seeking funds for their work from a wide range of sources, and applying these funds to their work in the most effective and efficient manner. They will also constantly review, monitor and plan their work. They have to be able to mobilise the creative energies of a team including paid staff, Board members, volunteers, members and beneficiaries. They need to inspire as well as manage. In participatory NGOs, managers also need to know how to work with people rather than administer unto them. Many NGOs work in insecure circumstances, by virtue of having to rely on funding from external sources.

All this means that NGO managers have to be a unique breed of men and women. It is however recognized that:-the personal qualities of the unique breed need to be supplemented and complemented by the possession of knowledge and skills relevant to the NGOs activities, provisions and target groups, and to the tasks involved in the management of the organisation as a whole. The personal qualities and dispositions of NGO managers are not enough in themselves to sustain and enhance the work and development of the organisations, in other words: efficient and effective management and financial systems are essential in NGOs.

HUMAN RESOURCE DEVELOPMENT (HRD) AND TRAINING

NGO work is much more difficult and demanding than many realise, as managers do and staff moving from the private sector and public sector to work in them have found. NGOs often undertake projects of a very demanding scale and complexity with limited resources. Yet the myth that NGO work is undemanding lives on.

More and more, NGO management training is regarded as a distinctive task in a number of countries, agencies have been established to provide it, and such agencies are often constituted as NGOs themselves. The distinctive HRD and training needs of Boards, members, volunteers and programme beneficiaries are also being increasingly identified and responded to. This is based on the recognition that it is as important to have a well trained and effective Board, for example, as it is to have qualified and competent staff, properly trained volunteers and aware, able beneficiaries. Well trained and informed Boards are less dependent on staff and more able to ensure that they are properly accountable.

Some of these new NGO HRD/training initiatives have an international orientation. Others offer research and consultancy services to NGOs as well as training programmes. At the same time more and more NGOs are recognising the need to allow time and resources for training, both in-house and outside.

Funders are doing the same: indeed some training

initiatives have been set up at their instigation or with their active support and involvement. All that said, there is an oft—repeated view that too little investment is still being made by NGOs and their funders in this aspect of their work.

In NGOs, as in other sectors, HRD begins with being able to attract and retain staff of the right calibre. In part this means being able to offer salaries and conditions of service that are as adequate and secure as possible. Many people involved in NGOs agree that the insecurity of work in them is a major problem. Job insecurity in the NGO sector affects both men and women but not always in the same ways. Labour force studies in many countries shiny that women tend to be concentrated in the low-waged service sector, which includes many NGOs This may be one of the factors explaining the large number of women employed in NGOs which have generally emerged from the welfare sector.

Even where NGOs are contracted to deliver public services, as they increasingly are. This is not bringing an end to job insecurity in NGOs. This is because the trend towards contracting out such services is often being accompanied by trends towards applying market place economics to the delivery of public programmes. This means NGOs compete with each other and even with private providers to secure contracts Trends in this direction are well advanced in a number of countries They are stimulating a great deal of debate, not just about security. Many NGOs question whether human needs, issues and problems should be seen as "markets" within which competition takes place.

Funders and contracting agencies have key roles to play in this aspect of HRD in NGOs. From the subject of adequately remunerating NGO staff there has grown another debate, one that is about the general "professionalism" of NGOs and their staff. One view holds that NGO staff should be paid comparable rates with staff in other sectors, based on a recognition of the demanding nature of their work and to ensure the respect of their peers in other sectors. Another view sees NGO staff as people who should be selfless, poorly paid workers and dedicated amateurs rather than slick professionals. There are undoubtedly NGOs which have gone to extremes here:

"(NGOs are) now an industry in which lots of money can be made. For example some have budgets of about 1billion per year. The salary of some is kept in line with top government officials. (This) welfare elite (has developed) while (such) leaders are publicly condemning poverty..."

The debate is complex. Other issues come into it, including those of control, accountability and representation discussed earlier: "Many voluntary agencies have become generally centralised in power. Their directors have turned autocratic, and are not guided by any democratic process...There is very little identity with the people with whom they work... the very antithesis of that prevailing in genuine people's organisations... To the people (NGOs) are become middlemen... they are new breed of top elites, replacing landlords and moneylenders... often seen by people as exploiters and lies tellers..."

NGOs therefore walk a thin line between being on the one hand professional, and achieving it by paying adequate salaries and investing in staff development, and on the other hand, retaining their traditional values and ability to be effective and efficient. It is not an easy line to walk.

The NGO sector is inevitably affected by trends in other sectors in society, by labour market forces, and by prevailing social attitudes, which increasingly lean towards individualism. To an extent, NGOs have to live with these trends and are inevitably affected by them. NGOs, however, have to keep in mind the values and non-self-serving aims which drive them, and express them in all aspects of their work. These values are a needed counter-force, especially in societies where self-serving individualism becomes extreme. NGOs are recognising this.

Reviewing, monitoring and evaluating

Almost by definition, NGOs are organisations that are constantly changing and evolving. Thus monitoring and evaluation activities are of critical importance to them because they are the means by which change and revolutions can be guided, rather than be serendipitous or opportunistic. Monitoring and evaluation are also valuable ways of capturing accumulated experience and expertise that is all too easily lost when rapid changes occur either within organisations or in the environments in which they operate.

In addition, many NGOs recognise that carrying out their own evaluation and monitoring, as a matter of course, is preferable to having external evaluations, and all the disruption and uncertainty they can cause, imposed on them by others. NGOs are thus increasingly recognising the need to enhance their work by having their own procedures in place for constant monitoring and regular evaluation. More and more NGOs mount such exercises in respect of particular programmes and projects. Less common are wholesale reviews or evaluations of entire organisations, but these do occur. There is a growing body of literature and training related to monitoring and evaluation. A number of organisations have been established to assist NGOs with evaluation and/or with reviewing or generally reflecting upon their work, some national and some international in their scope.

The quality and extent of information made available by or about NGOs varies from country to country. Legal requirements commonly mean that while NGOs must produce and make available certain information about their work, such requirements are frequently minimal. Indeed sometimes NGOs are only required by law to supply financial information to the relevant regulatory authorities. As the provision of information requires resources, which many NGOs do not have, there is often a dearth of information about NGOs and their work. In turn this can lead to:

NGOs being accused of consciously being secretive about their work; NGOs unconsciously not providing or recognising the value of publishing information about their work. Neither is healthy and many NGOs are recognising this. But, as with other aspects of improving NGO operations this is an area where NGOs need the support and understanding of others: as noted, information requires resources. In turn this needs recognition on the part of funders that information, like training, monitoring and evaluating, is a necessity and not a luxury.

Like other aspects of NGO improvement discussed here, additional resources expended will in the long run increase the cost-effectiveness of what is done. It is a mistake to see them as simply additional, unnecessary expenditure, which brings no return. NGO Directories are a practical way of informing the public, NGOs, government ministries and agencies and funders about the work of NGOs. Depending on the size of the country, and the range and scope of NGOs, they can be produced on a country-wide or more local or sectoral basis. A good example is Solomon Islands which has an excellent directory produced by a network NGO. It provides much more than names and addresses (as tends to be the rule). It sets out a summary of the objectives and work of each NGO and is updated from time to time.

Shortage of resources, as noted, is one reason why information about NGOs, whether individually or in directories, tends on the whole to be scarce. But another impediment is the lack of an agreed basis on which to present information, including that required for regulatory purposes. It is hoped that the definition and typologies contained in this report might form such a basis.

Networking and alliance-building

Through networking and alliance-building, NGOs identify common interests and concerns, share information, provide support to each other and maximise the use of available resources to achieve common goals. They are in other words manifestations of co-operative strategies to improve the impact of NGO operations. Many NGO networks now exist at local, regional, national and international levels. Examples of these are the Third World Information Network (TWIN), the Third World Feminist Network, Developing Alternatives for Women of a New Era (DAWN), Disabled People's International (DPI), the International Debt Network and the Commonwealth Association for Local Action and Economic Development (COMMACT). There are also international NGO networks associated with the United Nations Summits of the Environment, Population, Social Development and Women. International networking is increasingly linking

NGOs in the North and the South on common issues. There are also networks which link groups within international regions: the Caribbean People's Development Agency (CARIPEDA) and the Caribbean Network for Integrated Rural Development (CNIRD) in the Caribbean, the African NGOs Self-reliance and Development Advocacy Group (ASDAG) in Africa, and the Pacific Islands Association of NGOs (PIANGO) in the Pacific are among them.

In the national arena networks, we have examples such as the Community Business Movement in Britain, the Association of Voluntary Agencies for Rural Development (AVARD) in India, the Development Services Exchange (DSE) in Solomon Islands, the Association of NGOs-Aotearoa (ANGOA) in New Zealand, the Development Network of Indigenous Voluntary Associations (DENIVA) in Uganda, and the Canadian Environmental Network. There are also networks actives, both nationally and internationally, in such fields as health, education, and people with disabilities. At all levels of their operation, the revolution in international telecommunications and information sharing, through the internet and information super-highway, is presently enormously increasing the extent and impact of NGO networks.

Funders are acknowledging the value of NGO networks, just as international agencies are recognising them through admitting them to international fora. While they are not confined to NGOs involved in advocacy for change, alliance-building and networks are proving to be effective for such purposes, notably when the networks extend beyond NGOs to link them with other organisations. Networking and collaborative relationships between NGOs and the private sector are growing in a number of countries, and there is no better recent example of the value of networking links between NGOs and other organisations than what was achieved over the issue of apartheid in South Africa.

APPROACHES TO PROMOTING GOOD GOVERNANCE

The 1980s and the early '90s have witnessed major political and economic upheavals in most regions in the world. The perceived success of market economies, the failures of central command and control systems, and inefficiencies of state enterprises have overturned the strong, controlling role of the state in previously publicly dominated economies. Concurrently, the abuses of authoritarian regimes have led to a search for more responsive forms of government. These two fundamental transformations which characterize much of the world have been described as "the establishment of open markets and the movement toward more accountable democratic governance."

This paper reviews definitions of "governance" and those characteristics that can be ascribed to "good" governance. We then present a governance paradigm that recognizes the importance of a national enabling environment as well actions at the local level where much of governance practice plays out. A key element of the enabling environment is decentralization policy by which responsibilities are transferred from the central government to the local level where citizens can more readily participate in decisions that affect them. However, citizen participation in local government decision making does not come automatically. It requires specific strategies to establish communication channels and build capacities of both citizens (and organizations that represent them) and local governments to engage in a constructive dialogue.

GOVERNANCE CONCEPTS

In democratic or democratizing systems, government exists to fulfil functions such as maintaining security, providing public services, and ensuring equal treatment under the law. The specific nature of these functions may vary over time, but in western systems it forms a contract between government and citizens.

The contract exists at a number of levels: the constitution defines the broadest principles of the contract, national and sub-national laws and regulations provide a more specific framework, and the contract becomes largely operational at the local level. Citizens participate in government to define the contract and to manage and monitor it. The concept of "governance" has been applied to the processes through which public decisions are made. Landell-Mills and Serageldin have defined governance as: the use of political authority and exercise of control over a society and the management of resources for social and economic development.

This definition emphasizes the political nature and the management aspect of governance. However, it does not define the nature of the relationship between the authorities (the governors) and the public (the governed). Charlick offers another definition for the USAID Africa Bureau Democracy and Governance program:... the effective management of public affairs through the generation of a regime (set of rules) accepted as legitimate, for the purpose of promoting and enhancing societal values sought by individuals and groups.

In fact, there is a mutually reinforcing nature to building good governance, described in Exhibit 1 as a series of expanding concentric circles. Opportunities must be provided to citizens to express their preferences for the quality and nature of services they desire. Management effectiveness and behaviour determine how well elected officials and staff provide services that respond to those needs.

As local government actions are perceived to be useful and responsive, citizens are increasingly willing to provide resources for services and infrastructure. Again, through transparent decision making and management practices, local government demonstrates how it is accountable to citizens in the use of public resources. RTI's governance paradigm recognizes the importance of the national enabling environment in providing a legal and institutional framework for actions that are taken by stakeholders at the local level. It also recognizes that important features of the contract between government and citizens become operationalized at the local level where citizens and local government interact. Thus, a highly supportive national enabling environment promotes a rich and productive interaction at the local level.

Key issues at the national level concern basic rights such as freedom of association; access to information (press freedom); representative government including levels of representation and electoral procedures; checks and balances at the national level among the executive, legislative, and judicial branches ; and an intergovernment arrangement of power, authority, and responsibility (decentralization policy). While some of these are fundamental rights imbedded in a constitution, others are subject to legislative development and policy formulation by the executive and legislators. At the national level, part of the policy reform role involves modifying the role of central agencies.

In centralized systems, the central government plays a strong control role. However, in a decentralizing framework, this role must be transformed to become more assistance-oriented. Attention must be placed on creating or strengthening national-level institutions that provide support to local actors. These institutions include national training and technical assistance institutions and financing mechanisms. National institutions play a vital role in building capacity at the local level and providing a voice for local interests. For example, as attention has shifted away from the central government "control" role in Tunisia, the government, with USAID support, has emphasized establishing viable institutions such as the National Training Center for Local Governments and the Municipal Development Bank (financing municipal infrastructure according to transparent guidelines). In several countries including Ivory Coast, Ukraine, and Slovakia, RTI has assisted the national federations or leagues of cities in assuming more active roles in providing information and services to member cities and as advocates to central authorities for municipal interests.

DECENTRALIZATION PROGRAMS

While much of the early debate about strengthening governance addressed the national environment, increasing attention is now paid to local governance issues for several reasons. Various sectors of society, particularly marginalized groups, can most easily participate in decision making at the local level because local decisions most directly affect them. Also, they can readily have access to local decision makers, in contrast to national decision makers who may be located in a distant city. Information about the workings of government can be more easily communicated to citizens at the local level, establishing a clearer link between participation and outcome. Indeed, many governments have embarked on decentralization programs to foster democratic processes. Even where formal mechanisms for informing citizens are weak, the effects of local government actions remain highly visible.

In the 1980s the government of Côte d'Ivoire embarked on an ambitious program of decentralization, creating 35 municipal governments in 1980 and over 60 more in 1987 because, paraphrasing the Minister of Interior, local governments could become incubators of democracy. Cynically, one must also recognize that these programs were created to focus citizen attention and energy on local problems to distract them or to deflect discontent about the national government. Regardless of the reasons, however, there is clearly a trend toward creating or strengthening local governments through policy and/or constitutional reformulation. For example, in the Philippine constitution of 1987 and the Haitian constitution in 1987, both formulated in the wake of the overthrow of dictators by democratic movements, local governments were created by specific constitutional articles, reflecting the importance attached to the role of local governments in democratic society. Similarly, an amendment to the Indian constitution in 1991 gave formal, constitutional status for the first time to local governments.

Decentralization is the primary strategy for transferring responsibility from the central government to subnational levels of government. It is a fundamental change in the institutional framework in which political, social, and economic decisions are made. Many scholars have distinguished among different forms of decentralization:

- deconcentration is the transfer from central agencies operating from the capital cities to field offices of these agencies;
- delegation is the transfer of service responsibility from central government agencies to specialized organizations with some degree of operating autonomy (semi-autonomous corporations or subnational units of government);
- devolution is the transfer from central government to autonomous units of local government with corporate status (units with a statutory or constitutional basis for power that is distinct from central government); and
- privatization is the transfer of responsibility for producing goods or services to private voluntary organizations or private enterprises.

In fact, a decentralization strategy is most typically a mixture of these three forms, depending on the specific objectives of the strategy. However, the devolution form clearly offers the most potential for obtaining governance and economic benefits. With the transfer of responsibilities to local units of government, significant benefits result in terms of accountability, problem solving, and citizen participation. Local governments with significant power can counterbalance the power of central government. Local public sector managers are more likely to be held accountable to the residents they serve because the quality and quantity of services they provide are more easily identified than those provided by central managers. Effective pubic sector action assumes that problems are identified and solutions are implemented to achieve desired results. Autonomous local governments that are not held to rigid centrally defined uniform standards are more likely to produce innovative, appropriate, and more efficient solutions. Similarly, local governments are better positioned to work with local NGOs and other voluntary, community-based organizations in identifying problems and defining solutions. Finally, citizens can have more access to public decision making at the local level. The cost to citizens of obtaining information about government performance is less for local government services than for central government. Spatial proximity facilitates exchange and negotiation between local decision makers and citizens.

Significant economic benefits also can accrue from decentralization: better allocation of public sector resources and better mobilization of resources to finance public sector activities. In a highly centralized system for public goods and services, there is a lack of reliable information about the costs of those services, about their quality, and about the overall performance of public sector institutions. This plus the lack of a sense of paying for those services by their consumers tends to overproduce in either or both a quality and quantity sense. In contrast, the allocation of resources to public sector services is likely to be more efficient under a decentralized regime because local institutions are more likely to be aware of citizen preferences and needs. Furthermore, local institutions are less likely to provide unaffordable (without subsidy) services because they are more likely to know the real willingness to pay (demand).

Local governments have a comparative advantage over central governments in two aspects of resource mobilization. First, local governments can collect more revenues that are "local" in origin, such as business and property taxes. RTI experience has demonstrated that collection efficiencies are generally higher for taxes that are largely managed locally than if those same taxes were managed by the central government revenue collection services. Second, more resources are mobilized if the assignment and collection of taxes and charges for benefits are perceived as being provided by local governments. There is a greater willingness to be taxed and to pay service fees that are demanded by citizens in the first place and are more within the control of beneficiaries of the services, or of officials who are accountable to those beneficiaries. Decentralization is neither a single model nor an all-or-nothing proposition. Rather, there is a gamut of solutions for addressing the basic issues of decentralization. They may be summarized according to dimensions of functional responsibility, access to resources, and political accountability as follows:

- functional responsibilities: clarify responsibilities among levels of government (what the public economists call expenditure assignment). For the local level, the role typically ranges from the provision of basic services (street sweeping, solid waste collection, and public markets) to primary responsibility for local development planning and provision of a wide array of physical infrastructure and social services.
- access to resources: assigning resources appropriate to the functional responsibilities. Experience has shown that increasing the volume of resources

available for local allocation is an important factor in stimulating public participation in service and investment decisions.

- political accountability: devising a system of accountability that encompasses appropriate regulation of local governments by central government in areas where it is essential and by downward responsibility of local officials, elected and administrative, to their constituents. In this way a greater degree of local government self-regulation is achieved through local political processes.

In reviewing decentralization experience around the world, one finds that developing countries have addressed these dimensions in different ways.

- Indonesia's Urban Sector Policy Statement assigns responsibility to local governments for all basic services delivery. However, at this stage in its decentralization program, the Government of Indonesia (GoI) has not yet given autonomous status to local governments. Most local government officials still consider themselves employees of central government and aspire to promotion out of the local government system.
- The Philippines has achieved one of the highest degrees of autonomy for local governments. Local mayors have been elected since soon after the end of the Marcos regime. The Local Government Code (1991) provides for extensive reassignment of responsibility to local government units (LGUs), ensures local selection of local officials, and provides for a system of shared taxes and authority to LGUs to establish and collect local taxes and charges.

- India has a mixed strategy for urban development with some responsibilities assigned to local governments, but retention of considerable control by state and central institutions. In many states, local governments do not control and have difficulties influencing state development agencies in selecting investment programs; the constitutional recognition of local governments, however, requires states to develop mechanisms to enable local governments.
- The Eastern European model has involved considerable re-assignment of spending responsibilities for functions never before performed by local governments, including social welfare, housing, education, and basic infrastructure services. However, central governments have retained considerable control over major tax resources, hampering the ability of local governments to carry out their new functions.
- The classic African model of decentralization was a legacy of the local government systems in the colonial powers before independence. While both former French and English colonies inherited systems in which there was strong central government oversight, local governments in Francophone countries are under considerably more central control than their counterparts in English-speaking countries. Some countries, such as Côte d'Ivoire and Kenya, have made considerable efforts to update their local government models by increasing service responsibilities and financial resources.

Partly as a consequence of the activities of international assistance programs and technical advisors, and partly through observations of other systems, decentralization programs have tended to focus on a few key elements6:

- Getting the expenditure and revenue assignments correct, especially focusing on the intergovernmental fiscal system;
- Getting the political and administrative systems in place so the local governments have sufficient autonomy;
- Getting incentives right so that individuals and institutions perform as expected and desired;
- Strengthening human resources, particularly in local governments, so that elected and appointed staff have the requisite skills to perform as expected;
- Fostering community participation and encouraging NGOs to become involved in local government so that government systems adequately reflect citizen preferences.

STRENGTHENING CITIZEN PARTICIPATION

While many countries have developed decentralization programs, RTI has found that the corresponding political liberalization policies that foster the growth of civil society are often lacking or may be weak. This finding is not surprising because civil society represents a potentially uncontrollable opposition to political elites. However, the development of civil society varies greatly among countries and regions. Latin America and the Philippines have a fairly rich tradition of professional and community associations that play a large role in political and economic life of the countries. On the other hand, North and West Africa have weak associative movements for cultural and political reasons.

In Tunisia, official policy has recently sought to promote the creation of associations (neighbourhood groups, NGOs, and others) and their active involvement in development, particularly at the local level. Although numerous NGOs and other associations exist, they remain relatively weak with few resources and little organizational capacity.

In Morocco, the associative movement has been more constrained, but a few NGOs are beginning to appear as partners with municipal and regional governments. An RTI researcher recently observed that urban areas in Morocco, as in other parts of the world, are more ethnically and socioeconomically heterogeneous than are rural areas and, as a result, pose more of a threat of instability to governments. Part of the response is to strengthen the capacity of local governments to deal effectively with rapid urbanization. Equally important is the active participation of civil society in decision making and service delivery as a means to give expression and release to citizens, both lower income and the well educated middle class.

Strengthening the linkages between government and citizens/civil society, the linkages being generally channels of information, is a key leverage point for increasing citizen access and influence. Through RTI's analysis of local governments and experience in governance projects, have observed that two principal strategies improve these linkages: creating linkages and building capacity.

Open elections are a fundamental linkage that provides citizens the ability to influence decisions. Other linkages exist as a result of legislation that requires the local government to gather information from citizens regarding their needs and opinions, grant citizens access to council deliberations, or inform citizens of a pending government decision.

For example, in the US, state legislation typically requires local governments to have open meetings ("sunshine" laws) and public hearings before certain key decisions such as budget approval, regulatory changes, and rezonings. In El Salvador, legislation requires that local governments conduct a certain number of open meetings (*cabildos abiertos*) in which citizens are permitted to express their opinions on issues. Beyond measures prescribed by legislation, local governments may take a wide variety of discretionary actions to promote more participatory government.

These include publishing budgetary information and establishing a long consultative budget preparation process, creating a variety of standing *ad hoc* citizen advisory committees, and creating local neighbourhood development councils as partners in service planning and delivery. The possibilities are immense, and it is in the discretionary area that the vast majority of innovations in participatory government are found.

For example, RTI successfully introduced the idea of public dissemination and discussion of local government budgets prior to their adoption in some cities in the former Soviet Union. One mayor appeared on a televised phone in show to present the municipality's budget proposal and answer citizen comments. In a Tunisian municipality, officials are consulting with neighbourhood groups to determine their service priorities as part of the budget preparation process.

While these innovations are readily accepted in the US and other industrial countries, participatory approaches often meet considerable resistance in most developing countries. Local managers complain that NGOs do not have the capacity to engage in partnerships, or that citizens lack the technical awareness to debate service options.

On the other hand, citizens and NGOs complain that local governments are too bureaucratic, are arrogant, and do not want to share power. Mutual mistrust is the standard. To overcome these constraints, which are often attitudinal, governance programs must be designed to establish mutual trust and confidence. They must demonstrate how new linkages can be built, and they must strengthen the technical and organizational capacities of both partners to engage in the process.

There has been much debate about where efforts to improve participation should be directed. Should it be at the national level first to foster a supportive enabling environment, or should it be at the local level, building capacity to engage in good governance? Clearly, this should not be an either/or proposition. Depending on the context and on the targets of opportunity, both may be suitable entry points.

In RTI's study of governance and democracy in the North African and Near East region, local researchers felt that most countries in the region were moving cautiously toward decentralization and political liberalization. However, social movements, such as Muslim fundamentalism, prevented governments from endorsing these policies more openly. Furthermore, lacking democratic traditions, particularly at the local level, government officials do not yet have the necessary skills and techniques to lead participatory government, nor do citizens have the skills to participate effectively. The primary conclusion of the study was that successful demonstrations of nonthreatening problem solving at the local level would build local skills and confidence, provide concrete examples for other local managers, and encourage national policy makers to provide needed policy support.

CONCLUSIONS

Decentralization is not a new concept, and, indeed, it has been present as a policy in many developing countries for decades. Many countries have longstanding arrangements of subnational or local government as part public governing structures. However, in many cases, the relevant issues is not the formal existence of decentralized structures but rather the degree to which decentralization has been made an effective policy: to what extent have resources and functional authority been transferred to the local level, and to what extent has decentralization become a tool for democratization?

Experience has shown that where meaningful resources are transferred, functional responsibilities are clarified, and accountability mechanisms are established at the local level, decentralization may effectively produce the economic and social benefits that policy makers intend. Accountability measures include an electoral process, local authority for personnel decisions to make staff accountable to the local, rather than central government, a minimum of legislated mechanisms that ensure public access to decision making, and information flow that permits monitoring and performance measurement.

Anecdotal experience indicates that within this basic framework, local leaders are willing to undertake innovative participatory approaches, understanding the potential benefits of open process. Indeed, the most fertile ground for experimentation with good governance practices is probably to the local level where the public can easily participate and leaders can most directly feel results of successful partnerships with the community. At the same time, experience has demonstrated that successful local innovation with which national policy makers are associated are productive means to introducing broader policy change.

2

NGOs : Global Governance and Development

In all its forms, civil society is probably the largest single factor in development, if not in its monetary contribution then certainly in its human contribution and its experience and history. Ten years ago, there was little talk of civil society in the corridors of power.

Now, the walls reverberate with at least the rhetoric of partnership, participation, and the role of citizens' groups in promoting sustainable development. Though poorly understood and imperfectly applied in practice, concepts like "new diplomacy," "soft power," and "complex multilateralism" place civil society at the centre of international policy debates and global problem-solving. This radical change in international relations bodes well for our common future, but it is also a highly contested debate in which questions abound and answers are in short supply. In reality, "civil society" is an arena, not a thing, and, although it is often seen as the key to future progressive politics, this arena contains different and conflicting interests and agendas. For their part, global institutions are still be prisoners of a state-based system of international negotiation and find it exceptionally difficult to open up to non-state participation at any meaningful level.

We may dream of a "global community" but we do not yet live in one; too often, "global governance" means a system in which only the strong are represented and only the weak are punished. Resolving these deficiencies will be an immensely complex task for governments, inter-governmental organizations, business, and civil society to undertake together over the coming years. In this chapter, I pose three questions: why has civil society risen so quickly up the international agenda, what dilemmas lie ahead, and what should the United Nations be doing to reconcile the demands of the different actors who will shape the regimes of the twenty-first century ?

Changing ideas about Development

There are at least three reasons for the resurgence of civil society in the international arena. The first concerns changing ideas about international development. In recent years, there has been a significant move away from what was known as the "Washington consensus"—the belief that market liberalization and Western-style democracy offered a universal blueprint for growth and the reduction of poverty across the world. Central to the emerging "post-Washington consensus" are a number of ideas that place civil society at the heart of the development policy debate. The first of these ideas is that a strong social and institutional infrastructure is crucial to growth and development; "social capital"—a rich weave of social networks, norms, and civic institutions—is just as important in these areas as other forms of capital. Second, more pluralistic forms of governance and decision-making are seen to be more effective in developing a social consensus about structural changes in the economy and other key reforms; shared ownership of the development agenda is seen as the key to its sustainability. Third, public, private, and civic roles are being reconceptualized and reshaped, in both economics and social policy; the best route to problem-solving lies through partnerships and alliances between these different actors. Fourth, international institutions require stronger public and political constituencies to support them; otherwise they will continue to lose legitimacy, with potentially fatal consequences.

Civil society is central to all these ideas, and to their successful application. Although the empirical evidence for some of the underlying assumptions involved is incomplete, there is already a consensus among the donor community that a "strong civil society" is crucial to successful development performance. Civil society has entered the mainstream of international development discourse as a topic of central concern.

New Conceptions of Governance

Picking up on some of these ideas as they apply outside the domestic arena, the second major shift concerns a quiet revolution in conceptions of international relations. When Kofi Annan talks of "new diplomacy," he is echoing a common perception that the characteristics of global governance—the rules, norms, and institutions that govern public and private behaviour across national boundaries—are changing in new and important ways. As economic and cultural globalization proceeds, the state's monopoly over governance is challenged by the increasing influence of both profit-making and non-profit private actors. Corporations and private capital flows react very quickly to the opportunities provided by an increasingly integrated global market. By contrast, the response of states and civil society is necessarily slow, fragmented, and messy, because of the demands of democracy and the need to negotiate among so many different interests. In theory, civil society can be a counterweight to the expanding influence of markets and the declining power of states, but in practice there are few formal structures through which this countervailing authority might be expressed, specially at the global level. Transactional non-governmental organization (NGO) networks abound, but there is no world government to speak of and few global citizens to constitute a "global civil society" in the deepper meaning of that term. The result is a growing democratic deficit in the process of global governance.

Despite these difficulties, it is already clear that governance in the new millennium is unlikely to mean a single framework of international law applied through a unified global authority. It is more likely to involve a multi-layered process of interaction between different forms of authority (states, citizens, and markets) and different forms of regulation (laws, conventions, and social norms, working together to pursue common goals, resolve disputes, and negotiate new trade-offs between conflicting interests. The early stages of this model of governance described as "global public policy" by some and "multi-track diplomacy" by others, can already be discerned in global environmental regimes, such as the Montreal protocol, and in international, cross-sector campaigns over landmines, debt, child labour, and other high-profile issues. Civic groups play a key role in all these experiments: over 15000 transactional civic networks are already active on the global stage, 90 percent of which have been formed during the last 30 years. This form of governance is messy and unpredictable, but it will ultimately be more effective—by giving ordinary citizens a bigger say in the questions that dominate world politics and a greater stake in the solutions.

Currently, civil-society involvement in global regimes tends to operate through networks of interest groups (especially NGOs), rather than through formal representative structures. This raises important questions about civic groups and their future role, especially issues of structure, governance, and accountability that may erode their legitimacy as social actors in the emerging global order. As I will show below in this chapter, it is precisely in this area that commentators are raising increasingly critical questions. However, the role of civil society is certain to grow as global governance becomes more pluralistic and less confined to state-based systems that are defined according to territorial sovereignty.

"It's good for Business"

In addition to these conceptual arguments, United Nations agencies and international financial institutions have become more interested in civil society, and more open to working with civic groups, for a simpler and more commercial reason—it is "good for business." International institutions have found that operational partnerships and a broader policy dialogue contribute to more efficient project implementation and a lower rate of failure, a better public image, and more political support, especially among key shareholder governments in North America and Western Europe, and research and policy development which is more informed and less constrained by internal orthodoxy. Given these tangible benefits, it would be difficult for any international agency to retreat from the trend towards greater civic engagement. The practical and political costs would be too high.

This positive assessment is a comparatively recent phenomenon. Prior to 1980, there was little structured contact between civic groups and multilateral institutions, and almost no formal non-state involvement in global regimes. Toward the middle of the 1980s, such contacts became more frequent and more organized, including the consolidation of NGO advisory or consultative bodies for the specialized agencies of the UN system, the formation of the NGO Working Group on the World Bank in 1984, and some early global campaigning efforts around debt, structural adjustment, and popular participation. Global civic organizing increased at a much faster rate after the end of the Cold War, with the number of international NGOs quadrupling to over 20000 in less than two decades, and other civic actors (such as international labour union federations and networks of professional associations) beginning to take a higher profile.

Successive UN conferences on gender, population, the environment, social development, and habitation provided a vehicle for these emerging civil alliances to test out their skills, and both the United Nations and the World Bank began to form strategic partnerships with key NGOs in ventures such as the Global Alliance for Forest Conservation and Sustainable Use and the World Commission on Dams.

The assumption underlying these partnerships is that "global civil society" can broaden democratic practice by creating additional channels for popular participation, accountability, consultation, and debate, thus improving the quality of governance and promoting agreements that will last. The World Bank, the United Nations Development Programme (UNDP), and many bilateral aid agencies have embarked on a systematic effort to increase their understanding of civil society and its role in these contexts, and to enhance their capacity to engage effectively with civic groups at both the national level—through planning processes such as the World Bank's Comprehensive Development Framework–and the international level.

However, towards the end of the 1990s, critical questions began to be raised about this phenomenon from inside the international institutions, especially about the role of intermediary (advocacy) NGOs as a subset of civic actors. Having portrayed civil society in earlier times as something of a "magic bullet" for state and market failure, it is not surprising that attention is now turning to the failings (actual or perceived) of civil society itself. It is increasingly common to hear senior agency staff, academics, and journalists echo the complaints of some governments (especially in the Southern hemisphere) that NGOs are self-selected, unaccountable, and poorly rooted in society, thereby questioning their legitimacy as participants in global debates.

It is not that the principle of civic engagement is being questioned; more that the practice of civic engagement may be distorted in favour of organizations with greater resources and more access to decision-makers in capital cities, perhaps marginalizing grassroots constituencies in the process. Current trends in the UN system illustrate this ambiguity of commitment: there have been strong declarations from the Secretary-General and others about the importance of civic engagement, accompanied by increasing attempts to formalize—some would say restrict—access by NGOs to the formal machinery of debate and decision-making, especially in New York. At the turn of the millennium, therefore, there are forces acting both for and against the deepening of civil-society involvement in global regimes. The dilemmas created by this situation provide a useful agenda for dialogue and action-planning among civic groups and intergovernmental organizations over the coming years.

THE DILEMMAS OF NON-STATE INVOLVEMENT IN GLOBAL GOVERNANCE

As a result of the political openings of the last decade, civic groups increasingly feel that they have the *right* to participate in global governance. Much less attention has been paid to their *obligations* in pursuing this role responsibly, or to concrete ways in which these rights might be expressed in the conduct of international institutions and the governance of global regimes. This is sensitive and difficult ground for both governments and civil society. There are at least four areas of tension.

The first set of issues—and by far the most contentious— concerns legitimacy and accountability; who speaks for whom in an NGO alliance or network, and how are differences resolved when participants vary in strength and resources? Who enjoys the benefits and suffers the costs of what the movement achieves, especially at the grassroots level? Whose voice is heard, and which interests are ignored, when differences are filtered out in order to communicate a simple message in a global campaign? In particular, how are grassroots voices mediated by institutions of different kinds—networks and their members, northern NGOs and southern NGOs, southern NGOs and community groups, and so on down the line?

In the mid-1990s, North American NGOs claimed to represent a southern consensus against the replenishment of the International Development Association (IDA), the soft loan arm of the World Bank, on the grounds that social and environmental safeguards were too weak. In contrast, southern NGOs (mainly from Africa) insisted that the IDA go ahead regardless of the weakness of these safeguards, because foreign aid was desperately needed even if its terms were imperfect. The "banana wars" of 1998-99 provide a more recent example of this problem, where NGOs supporting small-scale banana producers in Central America and the Caribbean found themselves on opposite sides of a landmark dispute before the World Trade Organization. On some issues (like debt or landmines), there is a solid south-north consensus in favour of a unified lobbying position. However, in other areas (especially trade and labour rights and the environment), there is no such consensus, since people and their civic representatives may have conflicting short-term interests in different parts of the world. As globalization proceeds, these areas will become the centrepiece of the international system's response, so it is vital that NGO networks develop a more sophisticated way of addressing differences of opinion within civil society in different localities and regions. Very few networks have mechanisms in place of resolve such differences democratically.

In cases like these, discussions often focus on the thorny issue of representation, though there are really two questions that are being asked: first, is representation the only route to NGO legitimacy in global governance? Second, how "representative" must an organization be in order to qualify for a seat at the negotiating table? These questions are often conflated, with results that make sensible discussion of policy options impossible.

Legitimacy is generally understood as the right to be

and do something in society, a sense that an organization is lawful, admissible, and justified in its chosen course of action; but there are different ways in which these things can be validated. Legitimacy in membership bodies is claimed through the normal democratic processes of election and formal sanctions that ensure that an agency is representative of, and accountable to, its constituents. Trade unions and some NGO federations fall into this category, though whether these processes operate effectively and democratically is another matter. Agreeing on some minimum standards in this regard is an important part of the agenda for the future. A small number of intermediary NGOs also have a membership base of this kind (Amnesty International is a good example), but most do not, and very few international NGO networks have democratic systems of governance of accountability. This creates obvious problems in claiming legitimacy through representation; these problems are exacerbated by the financial gains that come from serving as a trusted intermediary for donors who want to fund NGO advocacy, but who cannot make grants directly to every participant. This sets up an unhealthy dynamic, since NGOs in Washington, London, or Brussels have a vested interest in maintaining the role of intermediary rather than encouraging NGOs, especially those based in the south, to represent themselves directly. The financial implications of losing this precious status are one reason why criticisms of legitimacy touch off such a fierce reaction among northern NGOs; this is one of the rawest of NGO nerves.

In their defence, intermediary NGOs do not need democratic ways of sustaining their legitimacy, since their legitimacy is defined by legal compliance, effective supervision by their trustees, and recognition by other legitimate bodies that they have valuable knowledge and skills to bring to the debate. Since global governance is inevitably going to be a combination of formal and informal political processes, it is perfectly possible for NGOs to be legitimate but not representative participants in global debates, so long as they are clear on the implications of the different ways in which legitimacy is claimed. No one expects Oxfam, for example, to be perfectly representative of developing world opinion; only that its proposals on debt and other issues should be solidly rooted in research and experience and sensitive to the views and aspirations of its developing world partners. However, even if Oxfam conforms to these conditions (which is a challenge in itself), this gives them no formal rights to participate in global decision-making, since this is an area in which legitimacy must be claimed through representation. Non-membership bodies may have the right to a voice, but not to a vote. In this sense, the best representative of civil society is a democratically elected government, complemented by the checks and balances provided by non-state membership bodies (such as labour unions) and pressure groups of different kinds. The resulting mix will be very messy, but it is standard practice in national politics and looks set to shape the emergence of more democratic regimes at the global level too. The world will never be perfectly democratic, but it can be increasingly pluralist, and if that pluralism allows all interests to be represented and debated then a better set of decisions will emerge over time.

It is no accident that questions about legitimacy are being raised at a time when NGOs have started to gain real influence on the international stage. In that sense they are victims of their own success. Neither is there any shortage of hypocrisy among the critics, especially when it appears that NGOs are being singled out in contrast to businesses (and even many governments) that are even less accountable than they are. Nevertheless, the criticism are real, and must be addressed if NGOs are to exploit the political space that has opened up in the post-Cold War world. At minimum, that means no more unsubstantiated claims to "represent the people" and more concerted and creative efforts to change the balance of power in global civil alliances. This will always be difficult but, when different routes to legitimacy are confused, the issues are impossible to resolve in any sensible way.

NGOs: From The Local to the Global

Globalization requires both governments and NGOs to link different levels of their activity together—local, notional, regional, and global. For governments this challenge is somewhat more straightforward, since they have a chain of intergovernmental structures like the United Nations through which debate and decision-making can be linked, at least in theory. The situation is much more challenging for NGOs, since there are no parallel structures to facilitate supernational civic participation, and no civic representation in intergovernmental bodies.

All around the world, governments, NGOs, and businesses are already experimenting with "dialogic politics" at the local level, sharing in planning and decision-making to generate a better and more sustainable set of outcomes. These experiments are the local building blocks of future global governance. By laying a strong foundation for negotiations over labour standards, environmental pollution, and human rights, they offer the potential to connect ordinary citizens to global regimes. But this can only work if local structures are connected to more democratic structures at higher levels of the world system, helping to ensure that sacrifices made in one locality are not exploited by less scrupulous parties elsewhere. Recent tripartite agreements on child labour in Bangladeshi garment factories are a sign of the future in this respect, with NGOs, government, and business striking mutually advantageous local begains within a framework of global minimum standards set out in the provisions of International Labour Organization Conventions dealing with child labour. Other regimes could follow this example by embedding local agreements in a nested system of authorities that balance necessary flexibility with a core of universal principles. Getting things right at the base of the system is much more important than introducing new global institutions that are divorced from their local roots—an exercise akin to building castles in the sky. Until such linkages become the norm, NGOs will continue to struggle to make connections between their work at the local and global levels.

These problems are not helped by a tendency among some NGOs to focus on global advocacy to the exclusion of the national-level processes of state-society relations that underpin the ability of any country to pursue progressive goals in an integrated economy. There is always a temptation to "leap-frog" the national arena and go directly to Washington or Brussels, where it is often easier to gain access to senior officials and achieve a response. This is understandable, but in the long term it is a serious mistake. It increases the influence of multilateral institutions over national development and erodes the process of domestic coalition-building that is essential to the development of pro-poor policy reform. In addition, the constant appearance of NGOs in international fora, combined with the dominance of NGO voices from the north, reinforces the suspicion among developing world governments that these are not genuine global alliances but yet another example of the rich world's monopoly over global debates. The NGOs concerned may see themselves as defending the interests of the poor, but it is still outsiders—not the government's own constituents—who are deciding the agenda. Most of these attacks are self-serving, but the asymmetry of NGO networks makes such criticisms inevitable. For example, only 251 of the 1550 NGOs associated with the UN Department of Public Information come from the south, and the ratio of NGOs in consultative status with ECOSOC is even lower.

Addressing this problem requires a different way of building NGO alliances, with more emphasis on horizontal relationships among equals, stronger links between local, national, and global action, and a more democratic way of deciding on strategies and messages. Jubilee 2000 (though a relatively easy case because of the absence of any south-north NGO fault-line) provides some good examples of these innovations. In Uganda, for example, a network of local NGOs have developed a dialogue with their own government on the options for debt relief, supported with technical assistance from northern NGOs like Oxfam. The results of this dialogue were then incorporated into the international debt campaign. Research has shown that NGO networks can achieve their policy goals, build capacity among NGOs in the south, *and* preserve accountability to grassroots constituents, if they consciously plan to do so from the outset and are prepared to trade off some element of speed and convenience in order to negotiate a more democratic set of outcomes. Sadly, relatively few northern NGOs seem willing to follow this approach, though, to their credit, NGOs such as Oxfam and Action Aid have started to reorient some of their resources in this direction—as with the Uganda Debt Network, cited above. Perhaps the costs seem too high, in terms of profile lost and decision-making made more complex. As we shall see, governments can help NGOs to deal with these costs and encourage them to make the transition to alliances which are less dominated by voices from the north.

Constituencies for Change

One of the consequences of globalization is that traditional answers to social and economic questions become redundant, or at least that the questions become more complex and the answers more uncertain. The theoretical underpinnings of pro-and anti-free-trade positions, for example, are highly contested. We cannot know in advance whether one course of action will be better than another, whatever the theory predicts. But this is a far from theoretical question; what if the NGOs who protested so loudly in Seattle turn out to be wrong in their assumptions about the future benefits that flow from different trading strategies? Returning to the issue of accountability, who pays the price? Not the NGOs themselves, but the farmers in the developing world, who will be suffering the consequences for generations. Of course, the same structures apply to pro-free-traders too, but NGOs cannot use this as a defence. All protagonists must face up to the same question: in an uncertain world, what does it mean to advocate responsibly for a predetermined position ?

Humility would be start, which is a challenge in itself to organizations used to occupying the moral high ground. More investment in research and learning is also crucial, so that the alternatives that NGOs are lobbying for can be properly grounded, tested, and critiqued. NGOs are adept at saying "no, this is wrong," but not so good at saying "yes, here is a viable alternative." Yet, a politics of pure opposition is unlikely to contribute very much to the regimes of the future. One of the consequences of this dilemma is likely to be a switch from "conversion" strategies, the traditional NGO view of advocacy, to "engagement" strategies, which aim to support a process of dialogue rather than simply lobbying for a fixed set of outcomes. This will take NGOs further into territory that may seem obvious ground—building public constituencies for policy reform—but which has thus far been largely absent from their agenda.

A strong constituency in the industrialized world is a prerequisite for the success of more equitable global regimes, new forms of governance, and the sacrifices required to alter global patterns of consumption and trade. Codes of conduct to govern multinational corporations, for example, are of little use unless they are backed by large-scale consumer pressure to enforce them. Although governments and businesses can play an important role in building these constituencies, the major responsibility is likely to fall to NGOs, since it is they who have the public trust and international connections to talk plainly and convincingly about global justice. NGOs have always talked of the need to build constituencies, but have focused on problems in the developing world instead of lifestyle, change at home, playing on the idea that "your five dollars will make the difference." It rarely does, and what would make a difference (mass-based public protest against Western indifference, for example) is never given sufficient attention. Many NGOs have cut back their public education budgets in recent years (seeing this as an overhead instead of a core activity), while government spending is only slowly resurfacing after the insularity of the Thatcher/Reagan years. A deeper engagement in constituency-building does not mean abandoning campaigns or surrendering the power of protest. But it does mean a better balance between traditional forms of NGO advocacy, and slower, longer-term work on the causes of injustice. To support this shift, NGOs will need to develop a range of new skills and competencies in public communications, and work with academics, think tanks, trade unions, and others who can help them to develop and articulate more announced positions on issues like trade and labour markets, adapted to different country contexts.

WHAT ROLE FOR THE UNITED NATIONS?

Civil society involvement in global governance cannot be legislated into existence or imposed from above. Nevertheless, the United Nations has a crucial role to play in nurturing this historic shift, both as "midwife" and as "host," making sure that its own structures and mechanisms are open to participation and serve as role models for the rest of the international community. This is far from the case at present. Since many of the questions laid out in this chapter concern dilemmas of governance and accountability, the United Nations, as the body charged with negotiating and monitoring global standards, has a special responsibility to lead in this field. In its role as "midwife," there are plenty of avenues for action.

First, civic groups, governments, and businesses need a "safe space" in which to exchange ideas about the practicalities of global governance, and about the implications for the different actors involved ("safe" meaning a forum free from the accusations and counter-accusations that often dominate the dialogue). A large amount of thinking and research is going on about new experiments in global public policy, but it is fragmented and poorly disseminated, especially among civic groups themselves. The United Nations is generally a more trusted convenor than the international financial institutions or the World Trade Organization, and is well placed to host substantive discussions of this kind in the run-up to the Millennium General Assembly. As far as possible, such discussions should be based on careful analysis of innovative practice (like the Commission on Sustainable Development), not discussions of general principles. Civic groups need more support (and less uniformed criticisms) in developing concrete new approaches to governance, accountability, and communications in global networks.

Second, the United Nations can help to support concrete innovations in global civil society in three crucial areas :

- Levelling the playing field for civic involvement, so as to encourage participation by the broadest possible range of organizations, especially from the south. This will mean additional support for southern groups to develop new capacities and skills and to travel to global fora (perhaps as members of national delegations), restrictions on the number of northern groups at the negotiating table (by country, region, and sector), and decentralized mechanisms that relocate the centre of gravity away from New York and Washington.
- A greater degree of structure and order to the "rules of the game" that govern civic involvement in global debates, without imposing bureaucratic

rules from the top down, since that would damage the creativity and spontaneity that characterize the best of global citizen action. Codes of conduct set and policed by NGOs themselves provide a useful way forward here. The "Guidelines for NGO participation in the CSD Steering Committee" provide a good example, setting high standards for transparency, accountability, representation, and behaviour that result in sanctions if NGOs fail to observe them. APEC's "legitimacy determinants" are another example—a way of selecting NGOs on the basis of the degree of "helpful knowledge" they bring to the discussions. At present, these rules vary widely and unnecessarily, given that most intergovernmental organizations face common dilemmas. There are other ways of clarifying the rights and responsibilities of access and participation, such as an independent ombuds person to arbitrate in disputes between civic groups and intergovernmental organizations, or between NGOs in a network who may feel aggrieved. Humanitarian relief agencies, for example, look set to introduce such a mechanism voluntarily, after a period of intensive debate. However, such formal mechanisms may not be welcomed very widely, and may be of limited use in practice: they World Bank's Inspection Panel has had relatively little success in institutionalizing accountability, though it is certainly an advance on what went before.

- A voice, not a vote, for civic groups in global governance. NGOs must recognize that there are justifiable limits to their participation in decision-making, set by their (mostly) non-representative character and the legitimacy of democratically elected governments. The key to civil society involvement lies through a structured voice in global debates, not through a formal vote in the Security Council. The challenge will be to structure this voice in ways that promote a genuine sense of equality and democracy in global civil society itself.

Third, the United Nations can play an important role in promoting greater rigorous in the debate, in place of the anecdotes, prejudice, and confusion that currently predominate. This applies especially to the vexed questions of legitimacy and representation, where general statements, are often applied across the board of radically different types of organization, forms of participation, issues, and requirements. This obscures the discussion of practical alternatives, and renders governments and intergovernmental organizations vulnerable to the charge that they are using the difficulties of practice to frustrate progress on points of principle. A number of critical test cases will arise in the near future that can be used to experiment more creatively with the principles laid out above, especially the Millennium General Assembly in 2000 and the follow-up conferences to Beijing, Copenhagen, and Rio de Janeiro. The United Nations must lead this process.

NGOS AND THEIR INDEPENDENCE FROM GOVERNMENTS

The most difficult question about the independence of NGOs is whether they come under governmental influence. Individual governments do at times try to influence the NGO community in a particular field, by establishing NGOs that promote their policies. This has been recognized by quite common use of the acronym GONGO, to label a government-organized NGO. Also, in more authoritarian societies, NGOs may find it very difficult to act independently and they may not receive acknowledgment from other political actors even when they are acting independently. Beyond these unusual situations, there is a widespread prejudice that government funding leads to government control. In the field of human rights, it would damage an NGO for such a perception to arise, so Amnesty International has strict rules that it will not accept direct government funding for normal activities. On the other hand, development and humanitarian relief NGOs need substantial resources, to run their operational programs, so most of them readily accept official funds. While these NGOs would like the security of a guaranteed budget for their administrative overheads, governments generally only want to support field costs for projects.

Nominally NGOs may appear to be independent, when they design their own programs, but government influence can arise indirectly if the program is designed to make it more likely that government grants or contracts will be forthcoming. On the other hand, confident experienced NGOs can appeal for funding for new approaches and in so doing cause government officials to re-assess policy. The best example of this is the way in which NGOs, particularly the International Planned Parenthood Federation, dragged governments into adopting population programs. There is no obvious method to identify the direction of influence, without detailed knowledge of the relationship between an NGO and a government. Environmental NGOs may have either type of funding relationship. Conservation and research groups may happily obtain government funds to support their programs: some are innovative and some are not. Beyond these situations, radical campaigning groups may be unwilling and unable to attract government funds.

POLITICAL PARTIES AND ETHNIC MINORITIES OF NGOS

While a political party is not regarded as an NGO and cannot gain recognition at the UN, a small number of transnational groupings of political parties do gain consultative status with ECOSOC. There are also several groups of parliamentarians with consultative status. No problems have arisen with either group, because they have carefully avoided trying to involve the UN in the "internal affairs of states". Human rights NGOs feel aggrieved that the same principle is applied to them, even though one of the purposes of ECOSOC is "promoting respect for, and observance of, human rights". In May 1968, ECOSOC Resolution 1296 (XLIV) specified that NGOs "should have a general international concern with this matter, not restricted to the interests of a particular group of persons, a single nationality or the situation in a single State". While this provision was dropped from the revised text in July 1996, it is still applied in practice. On this basis, the Indian government can block the World Sikh Organization from gaining UN recognition. Christian Solidarity International also lost its consultative status in October 1999 after it had allowed the guerrilla leader, John Garang, to speak on its behalf, at the Commission on Human Rights. The recognition of minority rights is such a complex question that it is handled very differently in different countries.

In both North and South America, the minority communities who are descendants of the inhabitants prior to the arrival of the great waves of European settlers are given the privileged title of "indigenous peoples". The term has also been adopted in Australia and New Zealand and a few other countries. On the other hand, governments in various ethnically diverse countries do not wish to accord any special recognition to minorities. The compromise is that the UN refers to indigenous people, as individuals who have rights, and not to indigenous peoples (note the plural). This avoids recognition of any collective identity or any claim to the right of self-determination. The restrictions deriving from Resolution 1296 mean the organizations with consultative status are mainly global or regional coalitions of ethnic minorities.

However, special procedures have been adopted in both the Commission on Human Rights and the Commission on Sustainable Development to allow participation by a wider range of indigenous organizations. In addition, in July 2000, ECOSOC established a Permanent Forum on Indigenous Issues, consisting of sixteen independent experts, half of whom are nominated by indigenous organizations. Through a variety of complex issue linkages, these NGOs can be important in environmental politics, notably in the conservation of rainforests. While they are only present in the UN system under the auspices of the arrangements for NGOs, indigenous people are often keen to claim a unique status that is separate from and superior to the representatives of NGOs. As a result, their alliance with environmentalists does not always operate smoothly.

RELATIONS WITH BUSINESS AND COMMERCE AND NGOS

A few intergovernmental economic organizations do allow an individual company to have access under their provisions for NGOs, but this is only in cases where there are loose *ad hoc* procedures and there are no formal institutional arrangements. However, as with political parties, non-profit-making federations of companies, established for industry-wide collaboration and to act as lobbies, are widely accepted.

From the earliest days of the UN, bodies such as the International Chamber of Commerce, the International Organization of Employers and similar organizations for particular economic sectors have been included among the NGOs. Until the 1990s, they were not of much significance in the UN itself, but they have always been important in the specialized agencies. The more technical the question under discussion, the more the policy-making process will draw on their expertise. One of the outcomes of the 1992 Rio Earth Summit, the UN Conference on Environment and Development, was to draw companies into global environmental politics and hence more into the work of ECOSOC.

Sectoral bodies are prominent when questions such as energy or transport are on the agenda. In addition, issue-oriented commercial grouping have been formed. The most prominent is the World Business Council for Sustainable Development, a successor to various lobbies that focused on the Earth Summit, to promote environmentally friendly business.

The oil companies have sound environmental credentials in some forums, but not in others. The Oil Companies International Maritime Forum is making a useful contribution to the reduction of oil pollution at sea, but the Global Climate Coalition opposes reductions in oil consumption. OCIMF is registered as an NGO by the International Maritime Organization, and the GCC is admitted as an observer to the sessions of the Conference of the Parties to the Framework Convention on Climate Change. At the World Economic Forum in Davos in January 1999, the UN Secretary-General, Kofi Annan, explicitly called upon companies to widen their social responsibilities by entering into a Global Compact with the UN.

Companies that do so agree to endorse nine principles, covering promotion of a set of core values in the areas of human rights, labour standards and protection of the environment. Soon afterwards, global business organizations, several hundred companies and the International Confederation of Free Trade Unions responded positively, but only a handful of human rights, environment and development NGOs did so. There remains a deep suspicion among many such NGOs about the possibility of companies implementing commitments to social responsibility.

Despite the suspicion of business, some NGOs have chosen to engage directly in collaborative arrangements to formulate and monitor statements of business ethics. This has been done both on an industry-wide basis and with individual companies.

For example, WWF (known as the Worldwide Fund for Nature until July 2000) took the lead in forming the Forest Stewardship Council in 1993 and the Marine Stewardship Council in 1996. Each Council works to promote sustainable practices, with participating companies gaining the benefit of having their products endorsed by the NGOs as being environmentally friendly. Similarly, various companies are having environmental and/or social audits undertaken on an annual basis, by independent assessors.

NGOS AND THE POLITICAL USE OF VIOLENCE

There has been no compromise in any political system with the idea that the use of violence is not a normal part of the political process. In the UN, aggressive behaviour by individuals is sufficient to raise the question of suspension of an NGO's consultative status. In the exceptional circumstances where group of guerrillas wish to claim their use of violence is acceptable as part of the struggle against an oppressive regime, the group does not call itself an NGO. Their supporters call them a national liberation movement, whereas their opponents call them terrorists. Sometimes these groups gain admittance to intergovernmental organizations, as if they were the governments of recognized states. At the UN, they have never been classified as NGOs, but a few have been given a different status, as observers at the General Assembly and at UN conferences. Within individual countries, there are rare examples of the use of violence as a deliberate tactic, by groups that would normally be referred to as NGOs. A clear example is the Animal Liberation Front in the United Kingdom. They are simply regarded as criminals by the government and by the public, including many who support their goals. A commitment to non-violence is the best respected of the principles defining what is an NGO.

STRUCTURES AMONG NGOS

There is a great variety of ways in which NGOs are structured. The classic model is of a membership organization, coordinated in a geographically-defined hierarchy. Individual people work in local groups, which coordinate in provinces and then have a headquarters in the capital city for the country as a whole. Such country-wide organizations are called national NGOs. Frequently, the national NGOs combine in an international NGO, or INGO, which may consist of regional groups of countries and be capped by a global body. Not all the levels of the hierarchy need exist. Many countries are too small to have provincial structures. Smaller specialist NGOs may simply enrol individual members at the national level, without having any local branches. Occasionally, individuals are enrolled at the international level. On the other hand, in large organizations, the international level often seems relatively remote and attracts little attention, even among the NGO's own members. The group running a local family planning clinic does not necessarily know about the work of the International Planned Parenthood Federation (IPPF) at the UN World Conference on Women in Beijing. Nevertheless, such global organizations with their membership measured in millions do maintain a democratic policy-making process.

While some may hold direct elections for key posts at the national level, the responsibility to the membership at the global level is always indirect, via some international council or assembly of national representatives. It should be noted that one of the ambiguities about the term, NGO, is whether it is referring to a local, provincial, national, regional or global body. Until the early 1990s, the matter was generally straightforward in academic, news media or political discussions.

The overwhelming majority of local and provincial NGOs never engaged in transnational activities. Thus NGO, by itself, usually meant a national NGO and regional or global bodies were called international NGOs. National NGOs did engage in transnational development and humanitarian activities, but, with very few exceptions, they were not, in their own right, participants in international diplomacy. When they wanted to exercise political influence at the global level, they did so through the appropriate INGO. In the 1990s, there was a great upsurge in local organizations becoming active at the global level, particularly on environmental issues, because of the Rio Earth Summit in June 1992, and on social issues, because of the Copenhagen Social Summit in March 1995. Since then, the term INGO has not been used so much and NGO, by itself, has come to cover both national and international NGOs. As an expression of the new politics, various terms then were popularized to refer to local NGOs. Grassroots organizations, community based organizations (CBOs), and civil society organizations (CSOs), all came into currency. There is still an ambiguity whether these newer terms cover organizations that only operate at the local level or also include local branches of national organizations. Grassroots and community organizations clearly refer solely to the local level, but civil society has connotations of any level within a single country. Indeed, it has become quite common to refer to global civil society.

Linguistic usage in the legal atmosphere at the UN used to be somewhat different. When the UN was formed, any involvement of private individuals or groups in its work constituted deviation from the norm of diplomacy being the exclusive preserve of "states". Thus, a national organization, as mentioned in Article 71 of the UN Charter, was any NGO based in a single country. No distinction was made between an organization that covered a large constituency, over the whole country, and an organization based solely in a local community or a small section of the population. The lack of any distinction did not matter, as participation by either country-wide or more limited national NGOs was so rare in the permanent UN organs. Participation began on a small scale in the 1970s at UN conferences, on an *ad hoc* basis.

When the ECOSOC rules were changed in 1996, to admit "national NGOs" to consultative status as a matter of routine, the presumption became that a national organization was a country-wide membership organization or a federation of local groups or an umbrella group, that is a coalition of NGOs operating in different fields. As is common at the UN, practice has not been consistent: a few local NGOs have been admitted as "national NGOs" to consultative status.

The Rio conference also produced a term that has only been used in environmental politics at the UN. "Major Groups" refers to a system of categorizing NGOs from all levels, for the purposes of participating in UN policy-making processes. Hereafter, use of NGO alone will imply that any or all levels are included, while local, national or global will be used when the meaning must be restricted to that level. Terms such as CBOs and Major Groups will also be used in the appropriate political context. A minority of NGOs conform to the model of a global democratic hierarchy, in which any person may become a member. One variant is for the NGO to have subscribers or supporters, providing income, receiving newsletters and responding to calls for action, but not having any democratic control either over expenditure or over policy priorities for the organization. This is common among altruistic NGOs, promoting social welfare and poverty alleviation, and also among environmental NGOs. Another variant is for a specific status or participation in some activity to be a prerequisite for membership.

Thus trade unions are only open to those employed in certain occupations (sometimes very broadly defined). Similarly, professional, scientific and technical bodies are only open to people with the relevant qualification. Such organizations may then be grouped on a functional basis rather than a geographical basis, before they form national and/or international federations. Trade unions do maintain democratic decision-making structures (at least in principle, if not always in practice). However, professional, scientific and technical bodies have professional norms that override democratic norms and members may be expelled for violating the professional norms. A third variant is a religious organization. The major religions do all have complex hierarchies, from the local faith community through to global spiritual authorities. None of them claim to be democratic: authority is based on faith, a holy text, the charisma of individuals or a hierarchical tradition. To some it will be surprising to discuss trade unions, professional bodies and religious organizations as if they are NGOs. Indeed, the leaders of all three will usually deny they are NGOs. Nevertheless, they are treated on the same basis as NGOs throughout the UN system, with the exception of the special place for unions in the International Labour Organisation's tripartite system of governance.

Coalition-Building Among NGOs

Once NGOs do decide to influence public policy, they organize, in broad coalitions, specifically for this purpose. This means there is a large number of NGOs that bear no resemblance to the classic model of a unified hierarchy. Coalitions may take the form of umbrella INGOs, networks or caucuses. In the days when the main form of communication was by mail and even transnational telephone conversations were expensive and time-consuming to arrange, multinational coalitions generally took the form of institutional structures. Many international women's organizations, the International Council of Voluntary Agencies and the World Conservation Union are examples that date from this era. They are referred to as umbrella organizations, to signify the presence under the single umbrella of a variety of different NGOs that do not share a common identity. In the 1960s, direct transnational telephone dialing was established and air travel became sufficiently cheap for individuals to meet occasionally. Then in the 1970s the news media gradually used satellite communications, so that events in one place were shared around the world as television images.

These processes encouraged the formation of looser issue-based networks of NGOs to exchange information, mobilize support and coordinate strategies. At this stage, networks still required some degree of formal organization, with enough resources being raised to pay the salary of a network administrator and associated costs for the paperwork. The International Baby Foods Action Network was the prototype, followed by similar networks on pesticides, rainforests, climate change and other questions.

The advent of e-mail and the web in the 1990s then meant that the costs of running a network dropped substantially and individual people could afford to take part in sophisticated instantaneous global communications. The number of networks increased dramatically and they no longer needed any formal structure. Once a lead organization or even a lead individual establishes technical and political communication skills, a coalition of thousands of NGOs can be formed rapidly and their influence focused on specific targets. The International Campaign to Ban Landmines, the Coalition for an International Criminal Court and Jubilee 2000 are the most spectacular examples. However, the impact of technological change should not be exaggerated. The most effective modern networks still derive their impact from being coalitions of well-organized NGOs. Although communication costs are now minimal, it is still essential to have sufficient resources at the centre, even if they are provided by a single member of the network, for at least one person to devote most or all of his/her time to servicing the network. A variant of the global network is a global caucus. This arises when a group of NGOs come together as lobbyists at an international diplomatic event, such as a UN agenda-setting conference or a UN forum for negotiating on the formulation or implementation of a treaty. The caucus will be highly focused on achieving specific outcomes from the diplomatic process. The impression is given that such a caucus is an ad hoc grouping that only exists during the two or three weeks of the relevant diplomatic meetings. It may be accurate that the particular combination of NGOs having the particular political purpose will never meet again. However, a successful caucus will be well prepared and will carry forward procedural expertise, substantive knowledge, political status and diplomatic contacts gained in one forum through to the next forum, handling similar questions. Key organizations and key individuals provide continuity.

Women's organizations and environmentalists are among the most successful operating in this way. When we consider something as loose and transient as a caucus, it is perhaps inappropriate to call it an organization. Nevertheless, structured umbrella coalitions, networks and caucuses are all handled in the same way by governments. In the UN system, all transnational actors have to accept the label "NGO", in order to participate. They may be present under the label of the coalition or of its constituents or through both routes. Umbrella INGOs have consultative status and networks usually are listed, but caucuses rarely have any formal recognition. Coalitions that focus on policy outcomes in a particular country or a particular intergovernmental organization will tend to take the form of an umbrella organization. Coalitions that focus on issues tend to take the form of a network or a caucus, with different members being active in different policy forums. In global environmental politics, there is a unique set of caucuses – the system of "Major Groups".

The term was adopted at the Earth Summit, when *Agenda 21* devoted one of its four sections to "Strengthening the Role of Major Groups". The preamble argued that "one of the fundamental prerequisites for the achievement of sustainable development is broad public participation in decision-making" and this must be done as a "real social partnership" with "individuals, groups and organizations". The aim was for the UN to move beyond the traditional reliance on the established NGOs, in two ways. Communication must reach down to individuals at the level of local communities and particular sectors of society of importance for the environment must be mobilized. The following headings.

- Strengthening the role of business and industry
- Scientific and technological community
- Strengthening the role of farmers.

The choice of these nine groups was the arbitrary and

incoherent outcome of negotiations at UNCED. It was influenced by the personal concerns of Maurice Strong and by the lobbying of NGOs who were accredited to the conference. It is arbitrary to single out women but not men; the young but not the elderly; indigenous people but not other minorities; unions but not professional associations; business and industry but not commerce, finance and services; natural scientists but not social scientists; and farmers but not fishing communities. It is anomalous, but understandable, to emphasize one level of government, local authorities, when they have responsibility for all the Major Groups. Above all it is incoherent to have NGOs as one of the Major Groups, when *all* the other eight (including associations of local authorities) are represented in the UN system via the ECOSOC "arrangements for consultation with non-governmental organizations". This incoherence arises because many in the other Major Groups did not wish to be labelled as NGOs and there had to be a category to encompass environment and development NGOs.

In the Commission on Sustainable Development set up after the Earth Summit, special arrangements were made to allow for participation by all the new groups that had engaged with the UN for the first time at Rio. Any NGO that had been accredited for UNCED was allowed to apply for Roster NGO status at sessions of the CSD and later was given a special fast-track procedure for gaining full status with ECOSOC.

Although the CSD is constitutionally a standard subsidiary body of ECOSOC, it has developed its own procedures for relating to NGOs. Rather than each NGO attempting to exercise its participation rights separately, the NGOs are organized into the nine Major Groups from

Agenda 21. These categories are used both by the NGOs in their own caucusing and in the formal proceedings. In addition, the CSD has gone beyond the normal consultative arrangements to hold various types of formal, and informal, panels and seminars. Notably, each of the annual sessions starts with the appropriate Major Groups making presentations in special "stakeholder dialogues" on the different substantive agenda items for that year. In pragmatic terms, the illogicality of having NGOs as one of the nine groups of NGOs serves a useful function, in enabling any organization that does not fit elsewhere to be included. This Major Groups system has only operated in the CSD and in other processes that have been derived from UNCED.

THE GEOGRAPHICAL SPREAD OF NGOS

It used to be widely argued that NGOs were predominantly a feature of Western societies. This false proposition was derived from a mixture of ignorance, Western presumptions of their superiority in the Cold War and nationalist rhetoric from authoritarian regimes. All societies in modern times have had large numbers of NGOs at least at the local level. Under the most authoritarian regimes or in the least developed countries there are still self-help cooperative groups, community welfare associations, religious groups, professional and scientific associations, sports and recreational bodies, etc. Even Romania during the dictatorship of President Ceaucescu was host to the International Federation of Beekeepers' Associations. The presence or absence of a democratic political culture is one of the major variables determining the number of NGOs, but the size of a country, its ethnic, religious and cultural diversity, the complexity of its economy and the quality of its communication infrastructure are also of crucial importance.

Thus there are tens of thousands of NGOs in countries such as Bangladesh and India, while there are relatively few in Iceland or Finland. A particular source of controversy is the idea that the major NGOs are "Northern". Many people are still trapped by the mental prejudice that organizations have to be situated in geographical space. It might be a practical necessity for an international NGO to have a headquarters office in a particular building, but the location of the office in a North American or a European city does not convert a global NGO into a Northern NGO. Equally, the historical origins of an organization being formed in a particular country does not mean it is currently a Northern rather than a global organization. The proper criteria for assessment whether an organization is global are the location of its membership, the staffing of its headquarters, the sources of its funding and the content of its programs. An organization, such as Amnesty International, with 56 National Sections, groups in some 40 other countries, an International Secretariat from over 50 countries and an African Secretary-General is a global NGO, even if it started in Britain and has its headquarters in London. Due to the spread of democracy and the improvements in communications, many international NGOs that started in individual countries became global at the end of the twentieth century.

3

NGO-Government Cooperation

The cooperation between the state bodies and non-governmental organizations (NGOs) in Central and Eastern Europe (CEE) has increased significantly in the past several years. There is a well-recognized tendency among the countries to expand the scope of applicable areas of cooperation, to increase the available forms and mechanisms for cooperation, and to institutionalize the partnership so as to ensure continuity and sustainability.

The forms of cooperation include a wide range of tools and mechanisms. Primarily, governments have supported the civil sector through enacting a favourable legal environment for establishment, operation and sustainability (e.g., by creating mechanisms to enable NGO to utilize diverse sources of funding).

Governments and NGOs have improved partnership in the delivery of social services, and governments have increased support to NGOs through grants and subsidies. Importantly, some governments have adopted mechanisms to financially support the development of the sector (e.g.,

Croatian National Foundation for Civil Society Development and Hungarian National Civil Fund).

Parallel to the financial relationship and partnerships in meeting social needs, governments and NGOs throughout CEE have recognized the importance of having continuous dialogue and longer term strategies for cooperation and support to the development of the sector. Therefore, some governments have established separate units, offices or departments to institutionalize the cooperation with NGOs (e.g., Croatia, Hungary, Macedonia, Slovakia, Czech Republic). The role of these offices includes furthering democracy and strengthening cross-sector relationships, developing and implementing cooperation agreements, fostering dialogue, enhancing NGO participation in decision-making and supporting the development of coherent policies for the development of the sector.

Furthermore, public authorities throughout the region have adopted policy documents, such as programs for cooperation or targeted strategies (e.g., Estonia, Hungary, Croatia, Latvia and Macedonia) which help strengthen the cooperation and support. These documents differ in terms of purposes and goals; however they all outline the basic principles of the cooperation and promote active measures that should be undertaken by the government to support the development of the sector and foster cooperation. Estonia and Hungary have already implemented the first strategies and have been able to draw lessons from the process, which serve as a base for the development of follow-up documents. On the other hand, Croatia and Macedonia have just developed their strategies and are in the first phase of their implementation.

Although there are many positive developments in the cooperation between CEE governments and NGOs, the process of the development of partnership carries many lessons to be learnt and shared with other countries. While the mechanisms or tools for cooperation might be similar, the processes are different in terms of the purposes and motivations, the initiators of the mechanism, the challenges and negotiations in the process and finally in terms of the results that have been achieved.

This article will provide an overview of the development of legal and institutional mechanisms to strengthen the cooperation between governments and NGOs in three countries of CEE: Hungary, Estonia, and Croatia. The Hungarian legal and institutional framework for cooperation can be regarded as one of the most advanced in the region.

The Croatian "model for civil society development" which features three state bodies as promoters of the development process is an excellent example of a local needs-driven initiative, which aims to foster partnership in the fields of consultation, participation and funding. Estonia is the first country to develop a policy document for cooperation in the region and is currently developing a new mechanism for government funding for the overall development of the sector.

The article will cover the following issues:

1. The basic regulatory framework that supports the establishment and operation of NGOs and an overview of government efforts to ensure financial sustainability of the NGOs through creating tax benefits for utilizing income from self-generating activities and private donations (philanthropy);

2. Analysis of the innovative mechanisms for government funding to support the development of the sector;
3. Institutional cooperation between government and NGOs;
4. Policy documents for cooperation and development of the sector; and
5. Involvement of NGOs in policy and decision-making processes.

By providing a comparative analysis and highlighting the successes and challenges of the development of cooperation and the innovative examples from these countries, the article will aim to facilitate cross-border learning and enable governments and NGOs to select the appropriate models to foster their cooperation.

DEVELOPMENT OF CIVIL SOCIETY

An enabling legal environment for the development of NGOs presupposes the right of citizens to associate freely in order to achieve common interests and needs. An enabling legal environment sets a protective framework for NGO activities and limits the ability of governments to interfere with NGO basic rights to be established and operate freely. It also requires clear and well defined rules that support NGO sustainability and functioning. Equally important, an enabling legal framework contributes towards the development of cross-sector(al) partnerships between NGOs, government, commercial corporations. For example, assume a ministry decides to contract with an NGO to provide services in a certain field (e.g., establishing and operating shelters for homeless people), allocates funding to support partially the provision of those services, and requires the NGO to match the ministry funding and use other resources to provide the service fully. The laws can support this relationship (and the provision of the services) in several ways. First, the law could allow NGO to generate its own income (e.g., sell publications on housing issues) and could exempt such income from taxation. Second, recognizing the importance of attracting private resources, the law could encourage the NGO to reach out to individuals and corporations and seek their donations, through prescribing tax benefits for individual and corporate donations to the NGO. Third, the NGO may want to rely on volunteers in the implementation of its activities (e.g., volunteers can organize some activities for the homeless people during the day). By removing the obstacles to volunteering (e.g., exemption from taxation reimbursement of expenses to volunteers such as travel to the shelter and food), the law can support citizen involvement in publicly beneficial activities, such as the provision of social services.

Laws Governing the Establishment and Operations of NGOs: The basic NGO laws create frameworks for the overall operation of NGOs, by regulating the basic lifecycle of the organizations from registration to dissolution, including the type of activities they can engage in (e.g., political activities, economic activities, and participation in policy or legislative processes), the status of public benefit, internal governance structure, and the ability to join unions or umbrella groups. The Croatian, Estonian and Hungarian Governments have all enacted generally supportive laws for the establishment and operation of NGOs.

For the last decade, Hungary has been considered a leader in legislation affecting NGOs. The first laws regulating associations and foundations were adopted in 1987, which provide a framework for the establishment, governance and operation of these organizations. In 1997 Hungary adopted the Act on Public Benefit Organizations (PBOs), thus distinguishing those organizations that are implementing activities which benefit the general public, and setting the basis for tax deductions and other benefits for these organizations. The Estonian Laws on Associations and Foundations came into effect in 1996, and relatively few amendments have been made since. An important development for Croatia was the enactment of the 2001 Law on Associations, which replaced the much criticized 1997 Law on Associations. The 2001 Law largely complies with international standards and regional best practices. Importantly, the enactment of the law resulted from collaborative efforts that included government officials from the Ministry of Justice and the Government Office for Cooperation with Associations, representatives from local NGOs, and experts from international organizations.

All three countries recognize the two basic forms of NGOs: associations and foundations. The foundations in Estonia and Hungary can be grant-making or operating. Foundations in Hungary can only be established for public interest purposes; however, the Hungarian Government is currently proposing amendments to the Civil Code, which would allow for the existence of private-purpose foundations.

Unfortunately, the Croatian Law on Foundations and Funds from 1995 prescribes regressive conditions for the establishment of foundations and gives the registration authority (Ministry of Justice) unwarranted discretionary power over the establishment and internal governance of foundations. As a result, only some 75 foundations have been registered in Croatia to date (compare with more than 30,000 registered associations under the enabling Law on Associations).

In addition to associations and foundations, Hungary also introduced a third organizational form-the non-profit company. Under this form, any for-profit legal form (out of the six types which currently are recognized in the Hungarian Company Code) can assume a non-profit status and seek public benefit status under the same conditions as associations and foundations. Furthermore, the Croatian legal system recognizes the "fund" as a third organizational form, which is defined as a foundation, except that a fund can pursue its purposes only on a temporary basis (i.e., for less than five years).

As mentioned above, only Hungary has a separate law which defines public benefit status. Public benefit status distinguishes between organizations that are established for the private interest of the members, such as bridge clubs, from those whose activities benefit a larger community. Public benefit status is fundamental to the sustainability of NGOs because most countries in the CEE region use this status as a conceptual prerequisite to granting tax benefits (exemptions or deductions) or other types of state financial support (e.g., in Poland only organizations which are of public benefit can receive allocations through the percentage mechanism). The Hungarian Act on PBOs is interesting in that it introduced two tiers of public benefit status: basic and prominent. Organizations can obtain the status of "prominent public benefit organization" if they undertake state or local government responsibilities (usually by having a contract with a state body). Although only about 6-8% of Hungarian NGOs have this status, they represent good examples of

NGO-government partnership in the implementation of projects for the interest of the community that rarely existed before this mechanism was introduced in the system. In addition, prominent public benefit organizations receive higher tax benefits than NGOs who do not have this status or than those organizations with basic public benefit status.

There is no separate public benefit status as such in Croatia or Estonia. In Croatia, the public benefit concept does exist in various laws, but is not consistently defined or applied. In Estonia, as you say, there is a tax-exempt status which is the functional equivalent of public benefit status. Only the organizations that are included on a government list are entitled to tax benefits. The Income Tax Act defines the criteria according to which organizations can be included in that list. There are approximately 1,600 organizations in this list.

The decision as to whether an organization can be entered on the list is made by the Tax and Custom Board). However, the law also provides for the establishment of a Committee of Experts, which should provide recommendations to the Tax and Custom Board on every application. The Committee consists of 9 representatives of NGOs, mostly from umbrella organizations from different fields of activities. They are appointed by the Ministry of Finance after consulting with the NGOs. This expert committee was established at the beginning of 2007 and it has met twice so far. The existence of such a committee was considered a positive development, because it aims to provide guidance in defining what public benefit is. So far however, there are two challenges in its work: (1) it faces difficulties in defining public benefit as this concept is still new in the society and there is much "grey zone" around it and (2) the Tax and Custom Board and Ministry of Finance are not receptive to the suggestions of this committee as these recommendations are not binding for them. It is anticipated that in time, with some legislative clarifications, the situation could be improved.

Support for Development of Own Income and Philanthropy: Generally, NGOs can benefit from three domestic sources of income: economic activities, or other self-generating income (rent, passive investments), from direct government financing, and from philanthropy (understood as donations in time and money). Hungary, Croatia and Estonia follow a positive trend in providing tax benefits to NGOs to enable them to generate their own income to support their activities. Also the legal frameworks provide incentives to help NGOs to engage supporters and receive financial contributions.

Economic Activities and Tax Exemptions: First, all three countries allow NGOs to engage directly in economic activities, which can be defined as "regularly pursued trade or business involving the sale of goods or services." Income from donations, gifts, passive investment, occasional activities which can also generate income, such as fundraising activities, usually do not fall under the definition of economic activities as described above, because these are not conducted through a market-type transaction.

In Hungary, NGOs can also engage in entrepreneurial or commercial activity which is defined as economic activity aimed at or resulting in obtaining income and property. The law provides that the following is not considered as entrepreneurial/commercial activity: (1) public benefit activity, or in the case of a non-PBO, activity according to the statutory purposes; (2) revenue received from selling goods and inventory serving solely the public benefit purpose or in case of a non-PBO, the statutory purposes; (3) part of the interest received from the credit institution or the issuer of securities, or part of the yield of state bonds, based on the proportion of the percentage of revenue from public benefit or statutory activity of the whole revenue.

The reform of the Hungarian tax framework affecting NGOs has resulted in a favourable fiscal environment that supports financially the development of the sector and stimulates philanthropy. In the mid-90's, several provisions were adopted which exempted all NGOs from paying tax on income from mission-related economic activities.

For example, all NGOs, regardless of whether they have public benefit status or not, may benefit from tax exemption on the income from commercial activities which does not exceed 10% of total income or 10 million HUF (approx. 39,946 Euro). Further, organizations that have acquired public benefit status are exempt for commercial income that does not exceed 10% of total income or 20 million HUF (approx. 79,892 Euro), and those that have obtained the status of prominent public benefit organizations are exempt up to 15% of total income.

Estonian NGOs are treated in a manner similar to business organizations in that they do not pay taxes on their income, but on certain distributions. Generally, they are permitted to engage in any activity that corresponds to the purposes stated in their statutes and are not taxed on income from such activity. However, if an organization is engaged in business as its principal activity or uses business income for purposes other than those specified in its statutes it cannot be entered into the government list and will therefore not be entitled to the tax benefits.

In Croatia, an organization's income from economic activities is considered taxed exempt only unless the exemption will give the organization an "unjustified privileged position in the market." The Tax Administration, on its own initiative or upon the request of a taxpayer or other interested person, may determine on a case by case basis whether to tax income generated from an NGO's economic activities. It is not yet clear how the Tax Administration will interpret the "unjustified privileged position in the market" language of the law, and what types of activities will be considered to afford such a position to an NGO. An organization that is found to have an "unjustified privileged position" is taxed at the regular business rate of 20%.16

Tax Incentives for Donations: Hungary provides for tax deductions only for donations given to PBOs. Businesses may deduct 150% of the amount of all donations up to 20% of pre-tax income if they donate to "prominent" PBOs, which perform governmental services. For other PBOs, companies can deduct the whole amount of donations up to 20% of pre-tax income. Hungary also prescribes a combined aggregate limit of 25% of pre-tax income if the donor gives to both types of PBOs. An individual may take a tax credit equal to 30% of the donation to a public benefit organization or public interest commitment. The credit may not exceed 50,000 HUF (approx. 200 Euro). In the case of donations to prominent public benefit organizations, the tax credit is 30% of the donation, up to 100,000 HUF (approx. 400 Euro). As of 2006, however, taxpayers above a certain level of income may not claim any tax benefits (including those relating to donations). In Estonia, income tax is not charged on gifts and donations made to persons included in the government list or to a person who owns a hospital, to a state or local government, to a scientific, cultural, educational, sports, law enforcement or social welfare institution, to members of the "church-register" or to a manager of a protected area, up to 3% of the amount of the payments subject to social tax made by the taxpayer during the same calendar year or 10% of profits for the last financial year of a taxpayer dissolved as of January 1.[18] In Estonia, individuals may deduct up to 5% of taxable income for documented gifts and charitable contributions to the same recipients as businesses can donate to, including also public universities and political parties.

In Croatia, donations made by corporations or individuals to organizations pursuing cultural, scientific, educational, health, humanitarian, sports, religious, and other activities are deductible up to 2% of the donor's income generated in prior calendar year. The established threshold may be exceeded upon approval of the competent ministry. The Government Office for Cooperation with NGOs, the National Foundation and NGOs have initiated discussion around the concept of public benefit status and the necessity of clarifying the legal framework, in order to expand the list of activities that may benefit from tax deductible donations.

Legal Framework for Volunteering: Volunteers are critical to the success of civil society initiatives around the world. They contribute to humanitarian relief efforts, service delivery to underserved populations, advocacy efforts representing those with limited or no voice in public affairs, and provide other needed services. The

Croatian and Hungarian Governments and NGOs have come to recognize the value of volunteering and they have launched programs to support and promote it. In addition, they have also undertaken efforts to remove legal obstacles to volunteering and create a favourable legal environment for citizens' engagement and social contribution. Hungary adopted the Act on Volunteering in Public Interest Activities in 2005, while Croatia adopted the Law on Volunteering in 2007. The Hungarian Act created new opportunities for citizens' activism by establishing a new legal relationship and attaching tax exemptions and other benefits to it. It regulates the provision of "public interest voluntary activities"; however it limits the scope of public interest volunteerism only to volunteering with public benefit organizations, governmental institutions, and public or private service providers in the social, health, educational, cultural, and minority fields. While the law explicitly stipulates that it leaves intact volunteering in other types of organizations or fields of activities, this implies that the extensive benefits and protections do not extend to other types of volunteering. Because over half of registered NGOs do not have public benefit status, this law does not cover the majority of NGOs and their volunteers. In addition, the law requires those organizations that work with volunteers to register with the competent Ministry; and it outlines a detailed and bureaucratic procedure of registration as well as conditions under which registration might be refused.

In Estonia, a Development Plan for Volunteering was developed by the Tartu Volunteer Centre with the participation of several NGOs in 2006 and it was adopted by the Joint Committee for implementation of the Estonian Civil Society Development Concept-EKAK. The goal of this plan is to define common understandings and activities in supporting and developing volunteering in Estonia for the period of 2007-2010. The Ministry of Interior is responsible for implementing this Development Plan. However, in 2007 the implementation was supported only with 265 000 Estonian kroons (approx. 17 000 Euros), because the plan was finalized after the state budget for 2007 was approved. Due to lack of funding only limited activities are planned for implementation in 2007.

DIRECT GOVERNMENT FINANCING

The government approach towards strengthening partnership with and supporting the growth of NGOs can be also analysed through the financing policies it has developed. The issue of government funding for NGOs is a significant part of the efforts to conceptualize, rationalize, and organize the government-NGO relationship. Toward that end, all three countries studied in this article have designed a policy document (program for cooperation and/or strategy) which outlines the core principles of good partnership between the state and the NGOs, including the commitments in terms of government funding opportunities. The core values embedded in the cooperation documents subsequently served as a basis for more specific and detailed pieces of regulation. For example, the Hungarian Government, in its Strategy Paper for Civil Society in 2002, pledged to increase the amount of state funding to NGOs and create the National Civil Fund. Indeed, in Hungary, direct financing as a source of income for the non-profit sector has increased significantly in the past 10 years, and in 2003 reached the target of representing 42% of the sector's total income (whereas in 1993 it amounted to only 16% of the total income).

Government funding can be distributed through several traditional forms, amounting to three main types of financing: support (usually through subsidies or grants); procurement (usually through service contracts); and third party payments (per capita fees or vouchers). These funds may be distributed from the central level budget (through the parliament, ministries, lotteries, privatization proceeds, public funds and foundations) or through budgets of local governments.

Of all forms and sources, however, it is worth highlighting the current mechanism of government support to NGOs through the percentage tax allocation mechanism in Hungary, the Hungarian National Civil Fund, the National Foundation for the Development of Civil Society in Croatia and the new initiative in Estonia to create an Endowment Fund. What is important in all these initiatives is that they provide an opportunity for NGOs to gain access to funds which can support their institutional, core costs – funds which are hard to obtain otherwise. With the exception of the percentage mechanism, all other mechanisms have been created following demands by NGOs that there is a need for a more targeted and transparent and – indeed – creative policy for the support of the civil sector as a whole.

The procedural aspects of granting government funding deserve particular attention. In most CEE countries the mechanisms for distribution of government funding lack sufficient levels of transparency and accountability, and clear procedures. To respond to these challenges countries have undertaken initiatives introduce principles of good government funding in codes or regulations. For example, in Estonia a "Code of Good Practice on Funding," an initiative led by the Network of

Estonian Nonprofit Organizations (NENO), is currently the focus of consultations between the public sector and NGOs, and is expected to be finalized by the end of 2007. This forthcoming agreement will serve to harmonize the principles of public funding processes (e.g. determining the form and setting the objectives of funding, eligibility criteria, grant tendering and application processes, selection criteria, contracting and payments, and reporting, monitoring and evaluation). Croatia also adopted a similar code (described below) and is currently assessing its implementation in order to improve the procedural processes.

Percentage Mechanism

The percentage mechanism was introduced for the first time in Hungary with the enactment of the Act CXXVI of 1996 on the Use of a Specified Portion of the Personal Income Tax (the "one-percent law"). It is a form of tax allocation, which allows taxpayers to designate a portion of the tax they need to pay to a specific organization. The initial idea of the "one percent law" was brought into the political debate in the context of church financing, when in the early 1990s the restitution of churches required a solution regarding their public support. However, in addition to this, the issue of financing of NGOs was entering the government agenda. All Hungarian government coalitions in the past few years found it important to stress their commitment to the strengthening of this sector by targeting two problems: (1) Hungarian NGOs received proportionately less foreign support than NGOs in other CEE countries and (2) the distribution of state funding to NGOs was over-politicised. The central notion of the "one-percent law" thus became the possibility for party-neutral public financing of NGOs through a tax designation mechanism. The percentage mechanism in Hungary enables individual taxpayers – natural persons – to designate 1% of their paid income taxes to a qualifying NGO and another 1% to a church (in addition to NGOs, there is also a list of budgetary institutions, and as an alternative to a church, a special budgetary priority objective is named each year). Taxpayers may make the designations on special forms enclosed in the tax return. The tax authority transfers the amounts designated after the beneficiary proves its entitlement, and the designators remain anonymous.

After Hungary introduced the so-called "1% Law," Lithuania, Poland, Slovakia and Romania have adopted similar legislation. Hungary has witnessed over 9 years of implementation of this law. Therefore, one can draw some lessons learnt from its experience.

In addition to the reasons mentioned above, there are two other overarching objectives behind introducing such mechanism: (1) increasing the pool of resources available to NGOs and (2) helping to develop a philanthropic culture among taxpayers. However, there are several concerns expressed by policy makers, NGOs and experts in terms of whether and to what extent the mechanism meets these objectives. First, the potential group of "donors" is limited as only taxpayers, and furthermore, only individual taxpayers can designate the percentage. Second, it allows only a limited amount (i.e., 1% in Hungary) to be designated which in terms of revenues may be quite small compared to other resources available to the sector (e.g., donors under the traditional scheme of tax deductions are not limited as to how much they can/want to give to the NGOs). Consequently, contrary to philanthropic giving, the "percentage cake" available to the NGOs has a finite size and cannot be increased. Thus, it is not only that the amount of available funding is limited, but also the receipt of a larger portion by one NGO reduces the amount available to others. It seems that in the end a small cluster of organizations (e.g. those who run the best marketing campaigns) benefit disproportionately from the mechanism. In addition, the overall amount may be quite small compared to other sources of revenue as the economy develops. In Hungary it was found to be less than one percent of the total revenue of the sector. Although all taxpayers can designate the funds with no cost to them, only 35% in Hungary use this opportunity. Finally, the effect of the mechanism on philanthropy cannot be easily assessed, as there are no comprehensive research results, which can show whether the law has achieved its second objective. Individual giving has not increased significantly in Hungary. One study shows that those who regularly designate their 1% also give donations in higher amounts or more frequently. However, this may also mean that those who are more philanthropic also designate their tax percentage more often as this is the higher income and higher educated group of taxpayers. This raises the question of whether their philanthropic behaviour would be the same regardless whether the percentage mechanism exists or not, given that they are more socially sensitive and active anyway.

Despite the above challenges, this mechanism does have certain advantages. Specifically, it has proven to be a good resource for local and smaller NGOs, because it is easier for them to mobilize local support (although in terms of the actual amount of funds it has a bigger impact on the larger NGOs who champion popular issues such as children's care or animal shelters). It creates competition among NGOs, thus contributing to increased professionalism, better communications and improved image. Most importantly this was the first and major reason why NGOs in Hungary started to communicate with their constituencies rather than with the government grant departments. As a result NGOs have become more embedded in their local communities. In addition, the mechanism gives the possibility to taxpayers to decide on how a certain percentage of their tax money is spent (decentralizing and de-politicizing the decision making process), increases awareness about the importance of civil society and sends signals about needs they find important to be supported. The government also benefits as it is able to monitor the preferences of society and regain part of the "lost revenue" through other taxes, e.g., VAT.

National Civil Fund, Hungary

In 2003, the Hungarian Government established the National Civil Fund with the aim to provide a mechanism for institutional support to NGOs. The idea behind this mechanism came from the need to provide state support for NGO operational costs beyond the existing percentage mechanism. Thus, the National Civil Fund supplements the mechanism of percentage allocation in that the government matches the amount of funds that are designated to NGOs through the percentage system. 60% of the resources of the National Civil Fund are allocated to NGOs to support operational costs. In addition, funds from this source also support development programs (research, education, international representation). Elected NGO representatives sit on committees tasked with deciding on the distribution of the funds. Specifically, the Fund is administered by a Council and a number of regionally based Colleges. The Council is the strategic decision-maker, which sets the priorities, divides up its resources among the various purposes, and develops its other rules. It consists of 17 members (2 representatives of the Parliamentary Committee on Civil Society; 3 representatives of the Ministry; and 12 representatives of civil society: 5 elected from national organizations working in various fields, 7 elected on a regional basis). The Colleges are the operative decision-makers, deciding about concrete grant proposals. They are organized both on a regional and a professional basis; however, their exact number and composition is still to be decided. Colleges have 5-11 members, the majority selected from NGOs. In the first year a total of 28 million Euros was distributed to support the operational costs of over 3,500 organizations.

The introduction of the National Civil Fund was accompanied by great enthusiasm from NGOs. However, the first couple of years of distribution of the funds faced many challenges, which raised concerns over its real effect. This was due to the lack of carefully planned implementation mechanisms on the side of the government. It revealed that in conceptualizing the National Civil Fund the Government did not consider a concrete overall strategy to develop the sector. Even the uniquely designed NGO participation in decision-making bodies raised controversies over conflict of interest issues.

Specifically, the implementation of the National Civil Fund was based on application requirements which appeared to be too burdensome and rigid. As a result of complicated and not clearly drafted application forms, approximately 70-90% of the applications were rejected. The responsible Ministry for overseeing the distribution needed to intervene to allow for a broader interpretation of the strict formal requirements so as to permit a higher number of applications to be considered. Consequently, the decision on the distribution of the funds came later than expected, leaving NGOs with only a month to spend the allocated funds, which originally were designed to cover costs for more than a year. At the same time, the substantive requirements were rather broad and lacked strategic focus. Thus, it is questionable whether the implementation of the National Civil Fund indeed supported NGOs to reform and to strengthen institutionally. In September 2006 the State Audit Office found that the Fund faced serious transparency and accountability challenges as well. The implementation of the mechanism revealed that the Minister and the Council did not elaborate an overall strategy to develop the sector, did not elaborate performance indicators, and the criteria for support remained unclear.

Although, the funding potential of this mechanism is considerable, its impact on general financial sustainability in the longer term largely depends on the willingness of the government and the Governing Council of the Fund to learn from the challenges of the first few years and to revisit the goals, in order to improve the effectiveness of the system. For example, for the second year of operation, the Council successfully developed a more clear and user-friendly application system but did not address other issues which could help the Fund achieve its purpose, such as criteria and types of projects that should be supported.

National Foundation for Civil Society Development, Croatia

Until 2003, the Government Office for Associations was the main actor that distributed public funds to NGOs.

It used to channel funds to all areas of work of NGOs, from human rights, education of youth, health, development of civil society, unemployment, etc. Independent experts' working groups were created to review and assess the projects and programs submitted for public funding. Although Ministries had certain funds to support projects of NGOs, this was not practiced widely and the cooperation in program implementation and funding became more centralized and focused mainly on the relationship between the Office for Associations and the organizations. In 2003 the Government established the National Foundation for Civil Society Development (National Foundation) as a public foundation, with the basic purpose of promoting and developing civil society in Croatia and decentralizing the cooperation between the government and NGOs.

The establishment of the National Foundation was the culmination of a 24-month process led by the Government Office for Association. The first step was developing a proposal for amendment of the Law on Games of Chance and Competitions, which would create the material basis for the establishment of the National Foundation. According to the Law on Games of Chance and Competitions, which was enacted in 2002, 50% of the moneys collected through games of chance are allocated for civil society organizations in Croatia. Out of the 50%, 14.5% are allocated to the development of civil society. 96.55% of the 14.5% allocated to development of civil society are allocated through the Government Office for Associations to the National Foundation, which then distributes them for the program "Our contribution to the community." The remaining 3.45% are distributed through the Ministry of Foreign Affairs and European Integration for international cooperation programs.

In addition to the funds from the lottery proceeds, the National Foundation is financed through private donations, income from economic activities and other sources. The Foundation aims to promote the sustainability of the sector, cross-sectoral cooperation, civic initiatives, philanthropy, and voluntarism. Core activities include: (1) education and publications, (2) grantgiving, (3) public awareness campaigns, (4) evaluation services, (5) research and (6) regional development. Importantly, the Foundation is be governed by a Management Board composed of 3 representatives from the Government, 1 from local governments and 5 from NGOs.

The establishment of the National Foundation was seen as a critical step towards improving the system of public financing for NGOs. As noted above, it marked a shift from a highly centralized system, in which the Government Office for Associations played the critical role, into a more de-centralized system. Accordingly, the role of line ministries was emphasized and they remain responsible for the funding of and cooperation with NGOs within their own jurisdiction. In the same time, the Foundation focuses on supporting grassroots initiatives and programs that do not necessarily fall within the competence of any particular ministry. In this way a more equitable distribution of responsibility among government stakeholders was ensured.

To guarantee that grant-making decisions, whether made by the National Foundation, the ministries, or the local governments, are made according to established standards of transparency, a *"Code of Good Practice, Standards and Criteria for Providing Financial Assistance to Programs and Projects of Associations"* was adopted by the Croatian Parliament in 2007. The Code establishes the basic standards and principles for granting financial assistance from the state budget to associations. It applies to all state authorities and offices of the Government, which support the implementation of programs and projects which are of special general/public interest in Croatia. In addition, the National Foundation distributes funds based on the *"Ordinance on the Conditions and Procedure for the Allocation of Funds used for the Fulfilment of the Foundation's Purpose."*

The Foundation supports several types of programs related to its strategic objectives, including the institutional support program, which supports the organizational development or stabilization for a period of three years, but only for those associations registered in Croatia. A grant is provided to help further the activities of the association and for the performance of its primary activity. Importantly, the Foundation also supports multi-annual grants (2004-2007), which are approved within the program, in the program area of institutional support and stabilization of associations for the program related to the linking of associations. The National Foundation also supports separate projects and programs to foster research, cooperation and development of civil society on national and local level. The total annual income of the National Foundation for 2006 was 31.736.477 kuna (approximately 4,346,270 Euro). The Foundation granted 12.943.80 kuna (approximately 1,772,657 Euro) for the operational support programs of 2004-2006.

During the first year of operations, the National Foundation faced criticism about its process of grant giving. The criticism was triggered by the fact that the body which decides on the grant recipients is also composed of NGO representatives, so questions about impartiality and conflict of interest were raised. As a result, the National Foundation adopted a more clear principle on conflict of interest in the above mentioned Ordinance. The National Foundation has also developed evaluation grids for the tenders that guide the NGOs, but also the evaluators in the process of deciding on the grants. Importantly, to further remedy the problem of conflict of interest, the National Foundation introduced a register of the potential conflict of interest situations which is not a public document but upon request it may be presented for inspection to the representatives of authorized bodies. NGOs have highlighted another shortcoming in the rules of distribution of institutional grants. According to the current rules an association which has received institutional support is not eligible to apply to any other separate project or program tender in the course of implementation of such institutional support grant. Further, they cannot apply for another institutional support within 3 years after their grant has expired. NGOs feel that this presents an obstacle for those associations which would otherwise be able to offer more good quality projects under different tenders opened by the National Foundation. In addition, since only a few NGOs are in practice able to fulfil the criteria, the number of NGOs who can actually use this opportunity is limited.

Proposal for Creation of Civil Society Endwoment, Estonia

Although the idea for the creation of a Civil Society Endowment is still in the formative stages, it is worth mentioning as it promises to be yet another creative initiative to support the operational costs of NGOs. The Endowment was one of the proposals made in a political manifesto of NGOs prior to the parliamentary elections in 2007 that made its way to the Government's Program. The concept was created by the NENO through a participatory process whereby several seminars and meetings with umbrella organizations and experts were held and supplemented by Internet consultations. Currently ministries are studying the concept to provide feedback.

The proposal envisions that the endowment will receive around 20 million Estonian kroons (approx. 1,3 million Euros) from the state budget annually. According to the concept, the new Endowment will focus on 1) funding the operational costs of public benefit NGOs, 2) supporting projects that create a more favourable environment for NGOs, and 3) local projects that promote civic participation and cooperation between NGOs. According to the proposal the Endowment would be managed by a Board consisting of 3 representatives from the government and parliament and 6-8 members who will be nominated by NGOs and selected by the Joint Committee between the government and NGOs for the implementation of EKAK.

FRAMEWORK FOR COOPERATION BETWEEN GOVERNMENTS, PARLIAMENTS AND NGOS

The framework for cooperation between governments and NGOs has been institutional through the establishment of different liaison offices for cooperation and communication as well as adoption of policy documents on national level. In addition, in some countries (such as Estonia and Hungary) the Parliament has also played a role in developing cooperation with NGOs and setting an overall example for a progressive state approach to supporting the development of NGOs and encouraging cross-sector dialogue.

The Institutional Framework For Dialogue with and Support to NGOs

Hungary: Over the years, the system of communication and cooperation with NGOs has become institutionalized across the government, both horizontally and vertically. It started with the introduction of special departments dealing with NGO support in the line ministries. In some ministries (e.g. social and employment), special councils or working groups have also been set up (with NGO participation) to advise the minister on professional issues and strategy development. Currently, there are also a number of offices, which promote cooperation between the state and the NGOs.

First, in 1998, a *Department for Civil Relations* was established in the Prime Minister's Office, which now operates under the Ministry of Labour and Social Affairs. The Department was established by government decree, without any participation of civic organizations in the process. However, its first leader was recruited from the NGO sector and thus, from the very beginning the staff of the Department was aware and responsive to the needs and concerns of NGOs. The Department is responsible for initiating laws for the development of the third sector (e.g., in 2005 it was closely engaged in the drafting of the Volunteering Act) and facilitating dialogue with NGOs. It was responsible for drafting the Government strategies towards civil society. The Department also provides information about available European Union funds and supervises the implementation and work of the National Civil Fund. It is currently working to develop a nationwide database system for NGOs, which is lacking in Hungary.

More recently, a special department was set up in the Ministry for Local Governments and Regional Development, which also houses the National Development Agency (responsible for implementing the European Union National Plans and Structural Fund Programs), called the *Department for Social Dialogue*, which is responsible for coordinating involvement of NGOs and other social partners in the development, implementation and monitoring of European Union instruments in Hungary.

Furthermore, practically every Ministry has by now set up a *contact office* or at least a *person responsible for liaising with civic organizations.* As ministries engage in more and more intensive working relationships with NGOs, they each develop their own internal rules and systems to support NGOs and involve them in decision-making processes.

Regarding the Parliament, a *Parliamentary Committee for the Support of Civil Organizations* existed from the early 1990s until 2006. It used to grant budget subsidies to national associations and with the institutionalization of the National Civil Fund, which overtook the grant giving role, this Committee took on the responsibility for legislative policy concerning the sector. In 2006, however, it was merged with the Committee on Human Rights, Religion and Minorities.

In addition, a *Civil Office of the Parliament* also continues to exist, which fulfils an informational role; e.g. maintains a database of NGOs to which it sends out the Parliament's legislative agenda sorted by area of interest (e.g. if an NGO wants to receive the legislative plans on environment related laws, they can sign up for such option); answers NGO inquiries; coordinates and arranges

NGO participation in the various Committee meetings etc.

Croatia: The institutionalization of the NGO-Government cooperation in Croatia commenced with the establishment of the *Government Office for Associations*, a centralized NGO liaison office on the Government level. Subsequently, the Government established *the Council for Development of Civil Society* (the Council) which works in partnership with the office. The cooperation between the two sectors proved to be a vibrant process that was flexible to adjust to the current needs of the two sectors. In 2002, the Government promised to submit a proposal for financing NGOs to the Croatian Parliament. The Government Office for Associations immediately embarked on this initiative and developed plans for a decentralized system of funding and cooperation. As a result, the framework of the New Model of the Organizational Structure for Civil Society Development in Croatia ("the new model") was established. This model consists of three bodies: the Office for Associations, the Council and the National Foundation for Civil Society Development (described above). The model also envisioned the creation of a Strategy for the Development of the Civil Society (which was adopted in 2006) and harmonization of the state funding process.

As mentioned above, the introduction of this model was triggered by the need to support direct communication between various Ministries and NGOs, in order to enhance their cooperation in addressing particular social needs. Until then, the NGO-Government cooperation was mainly centralized and was functioning effectively only between the Office for Associations and NGOs. The relationship with the other states bodies was not so developed. The new model also opened the possibilities of diversifying funding sources for NGOs and of tapping alternative and matching funds for joint NGO-government activities. The new model increased the cooperation between different ministries and NGOs and it encouraged Ministries to designate a person or unit responsible for fostering cooperating and dialogue with NGOs.

The Government Office for Cooperation with Associations was established in October 1998 by the Act of Government of Republic Croatia. The Office for NGOs was primarily entrusted with the task of building confidence and developing cooperation through financing, consulting, educating and information sharing. It also coordinated working groups on various legislative initiatives affecting NGOs, such as the Law on Associations, the Law on Income from Games of Chance and Competitions, the Law on Volunteers etc. Most importantly, the Office for Associations achieved remarkable results in drafting and implementing a transparent national program for public financing of NGOs. The Office for Associations channelled funds in all areas of work of NGOs, from human rights, to education of youth, health, development of civil society, unemployment, etc. Working groups of independent experts were created to review and assess the projects and programs submitted for public funding. During the period 1999-2003, 1,997 programs and projects were funded in the total amount of approximately 13,830,004 Euros. With the opening of the Office for Associations, a new era began in the relationship between the Government and NGOs and a new incentive was given for the further development of cooperation.

A further step in the advancement of collaboration

between the government and NGOs in Croatia was the establishment of the *Council for the Development of Civil Society* as a governmental advisory body in 2002. The Council is composed of 10 representatives from the Ministries and 14 representatives of civil society (elected by the NGOs themselves). The Council focuses its activities on the implementation of the Strategy for the Development of Civil Society and harmonization and oversight of financial support provided from the State budget for financing NGOs programs/projects. The role of the Council is to provide advice to the Government regarding NGO development and policies, as well as to coordinate efforts in realizing goals and action plans developed in the *"National Strategy for Creating Supportive Environment for the Development of Civil Society."* The Council has no veto power over Government's decisions, but can initiate different discussions important for civil society development and oversee the implementation of policies and strategies. In past years it was proven that the work of the Council seems to depend greatly upon the motivation of its members and, especially its President.

As mentioned above the third body in this model is the *National Foundation for Civil Society Development*. In addition to grant mechanisms, it also runs educational, training and research programs. Its goals focus on (1) the encouragement of public action, inclusion and participation in community development, (2) building capacity of civil society organizations, (3) the development of inter-sectoral cooperation and cooperation between civil society organizations, (4) increasing public influence and the visibility of the work of NGOs, (5) the development of social enterprise and employment in the not-for-profit sector and (6) increasing the influence of the civil society in the process of adoption of public policies. The National

Foundation cooperates with all three sectors of the society: public authorities, business and NGOs. In 2007, the National Foundation selected, through a public competition, three organizations and their network of organizations, located in three major regions in Croatia, with whom it will cooperate in the process of financing, regional development and capacity building of the third sector. This initiative was one of the efforts of the National Foundation to decentralize further the cooperation and financing schemes. The National Foundation has participated in many legislative drafting initiatives aiming to improve the legal framework for NGOs and conducted significant research on issues relevant for the Croatian NGOs.

In addition, with property granted by the Government, the National Foundation established the *European Centre for Cross-Sectoral Partnerships (IMPACT)* in Zadar, which aims to become a European center of excellence in education and training for representatives of all three sectors in society, for innovative and sustainable programs of inter-sectoral cooperation.

Estonia: In Estonia, the *Minister of Regional Affairs* is responsible for the development of civil society (together with his other duties that include public services and regional policy). The Minister's staff in the field of civil society is limited to two full-time officials dealing with civil society issues and two political advisers. Although the Minister has declared a plan to form a department for civil society, the concept of such department has to date not been developed. Other Ministries cooperate with NGOs as well; however the extent of this co-operation can vary considerably. Notable examples include the Ministries of Foreign Affairs, Economic Affairs, Culture,

Finance, Education, and Social Affairs. In addition, *the Government Communication Office at the State Chancellery* is also engaged actively with fostering the culture of public participation among public authorities. In addition, in 2007 each ministry named an official who is responsible for organizing public involvement in law-making processes.

A *parliamentary group for the support of civil society* is also formed in Riigikogu (Estonian parliament) that includes representatives from all political parties in the Parliament. More than one-third of MPs belong to this group, thus making it the biggest parliamentary grouping in Riigikogu. The group perceives its role to be discussion of the situation and initiation of necessary legislation for support of civil society development. However, they have not made legislative initiatives or statements so far.

Policy Documents on Cooperation with NGOs

Policy documents on cooperation with NGOs express the position of public authorities on the role of NGOs in society and the commitment for future constructive interaction with them. Such documents outline the principles of cooperation, they provide for a means for NGOs to receive increased support for their work and hence, to expand the areas of their activity in the interest of society and opportunities for partnerships in initiatives for addressing common needs.

Since they all aim to promote partnership and dialogue, it is also important that all of them are developed through a highly participatory process and the involvement of NGOs. All three countries analysed in this article have developed such policy documents, and all of them have been able to evaluate their implementation.

Croatian Program of Cooperation and Strategy: The first document between the Croatian Government and NGOs was the *"Program of Cooperation between the Government of the Republic of Croatia and the Non-Governmental, Non-Profit Sector"* which was signed in 2001.48 The Program of Cooperation is based on "common values of modern democracy and the values of civic initiatives founded on social changes, cooperation, solidarity, social justice, transparency, personal ability and responsibility, participation in decision-making, consideration for personality, self-organisation, consideration for organizational diversity and continuous learning. It aims to create effective mechanisms that will enhance the communication between the Government and the Sector." Although the Program for Cooperation listed the obligations of the Government and NGOs, it was not perceived as a legally binding document. The Program was conceived as a living document – "a starting point, not a conclusion" – with an "authority evolved from the confirmation" given by both sides. Additionally, the Program of Cooperation anticipated the creation of local and regional compacts so as to decentralize cross-sectoral cooperation. The implementation of the Program of Cooperation has been evaluated positively. It led to legislative reforms benefiting NGOs, including the new Law on Associations, the Lottery Law, the Law on Volunteerism and draft Law on Foundations, the Code of Good Practice in Grant-Giving, tax law amendments providing deductions for donations to NGOs, and the creation of local compacts in cities throughout Croatia.

Following the successful implementation of the Program for Cooperation, the Croatian Government adopted in 2006 a *"National Strategy for Creating Supportive Environment for the Development of Civil*

Society." The Strategy outlines the goals and measures that should be accomplished by 2011 in order to increase and strengthen the legal, financial and institutional framework for the support of civil society. Specifically, the Strategy contains targeted objectives and measures in the fields of participation in decision-making, the legal and tax framework for NGOs, the institutional framework for cooperation, financing of NGOs through contracting, development of social enterprises, development of philanthropy, volunteering and foundations, social cohesion, and the role of NGOs in the process of European Union integration. The Strategy was developed through a highly consultative, collaborative and participatory process by NGOs and government officials. Upon the adoption of the Strategy the Office for Associations developed an Operational Plan for Implementation of the Strategy which was adopted by the Government in February 2007. The Operational Plan clearly outlines all the measures necessary to support the implementation of the Strategic goals, the deadlines and the responsible ministries or state bodies.

Strategy Paper of the Government of Hungary on Civil Society: In 2002, the Department for Civil Relations led the process of development of a Strategy Paper of the Government of Hungary on Civil Society. The Strategy was initiated as a result of the fact that the then newly-elected government made cooperation and communication with civil organizations a priority objective. The elaboration of the policy document and consequent legislation was put on the fast track and its development was – though contentious-highly participatory. Comments from the NGOs were considered and mostly integrated into the final document. Initially, the government actually envisioned the signing of a "real" compact type agreement with the representatives of the NGO sector, which would have required a single representative body of the NGOs to sign it. Since there was strong resistance among civil society organizations against such a notion of a single representative body of NGOs, the government had to abandon this idea.

In terms of its implementation, the Hungarian Government has accomplished the central idea of the Government Strategy, that being the establishment of the National Civil Fund and also has made progress in its legislative plans, especially by adopting the Law on Volunteering.

In 2006 the Government launched a process of developing a new strategy for its partnership with civil society. At this time, however, instead of developing one central strategic document for the whole Government, the Ministries were entrusted with developing their own separate strategies, to help decentralize the cooperation and make it more effective. Besides the Ministry documents, a second Governmental Strategy was also developed and adopted in 2007.

Estonian Civil Society Development Concept and Civic Initiative Support Development Plan: The Estonian *Civil Society Development Concept-EKAK* is perhaps the only policy document adopted by a Parliament in CEE. EKAK was adopted in 2002 and a joint committee for its implementation was created in order to advance the implementation goals of EKAK. EKAK reflects the following priorities for development of the sector: sustainability, accountability, and transparency mechanisms for civil society. The national priorities are reflected in EKAK activities, which are designed to address issues of great concern to both the public and voluntary sectors, including legislation regulating citizen initiatives, involvement of citizens and citizens' associations in decision-making processes, financing of citizens' associations, compilation of statistics on the NGO sector's size and activities, civic education, and public awareness. The Estonian EKAK has its own Implementation Plan, and the implementation schedule is followed strictly by both parties. The EKAK implementation plan formulates goals, activities to achieve each goal, and specific indicators to measure achievement. It allocates responsibilities and contains a fixed schedule. Although the implementation plan was drafted in pursuit of the EKAK's short-term priorities, it also came as a result of the government's and the non-profit sector's joint efforts and understanding of the essential aspects of civic, legislative, and economic life in the country and the importance of adopting a comprehensive approach to solving problems in these areas. The Estonian EKAK resulted from bilateral initiatives and nationwide public discussions.

"The process of writing, rewriting and once again rewriting the document also became an international success story. Kristina Mänd, executive director of NENO, recalls how an Indian rose from his seat at a meeting in Canada, which the country's NGOs, politicians and public officials had summoned, slapped his fist on the table and told Canadian officials: "If you can't do it like Estonians, don't do it at all!" Unlike the Estonians, the Canadians felt that they had been pushed too far into the background when a similar Canadian document, the Accord, was discussed. Indeed, even before the concept was adopted by the Riigikogu, Estonian NGOs had talked about the paper in the USA, Canada, Japan, Hungary, Ukraine, Australia, Denmark, the Czech Republic, Germany, Poland, Russia, Latvia, Lithuania, South-Africa, Brussels, Strasbourg...

Everywhere it became a "best practice" and was cited with excitement. According to program manager Daimar Liiv, who coordinated the completion of the document, it is the first cooperation document of its kind approved by a country's parliament. "It demonstrates to the world that a political agreement has been reached in Estonia between the NGO sector and the state over how to enhance cooperation," Liiv says. Writing the document and seeing it adopted by the parliament gave the national NGO community a boost of self-esteem."

A Joint Committee was established in 2003 composed of representatives of each ministry and civil society. Among other things, the Committee was assigned to evaluate the degree to which the parties have fulfilled the commitments they undertook in the EKAK, as well as to develop an Implementation Plan for future action. Thus, while created in execution of the EKAK, this body has served as a link between various stages of the adoption and implementation processes. Importantly, the work of the Committee enabled the two sectors to reach a higher level of collaboration.

In the years following the establishment of the Committee, membership increased to 30, which slowed down the efficiency of the work of the Committee. At the end of 2006, NENO conducted an audit for the joint committee that identified three main problems in implementing EKAK: (1) lack of political interest; (2) poor quality and implementation of activity plans caused by insufficient financial and human resources, and (3) unclear role and responsibilities of both the committee and its members, especially from the side of public sector (the ministries were represented by officials who usually didn't have the power to make decisions in the name of the ministry). In order to solve these problems, NGOs recommended the revision of the principles and membership of the Joint Committee and formation of implementation units in both the public sector and NGOs. During the summer of 2007, the principles and membership of the Committee were revised, and as a result the new committee is smaller in number, but composed of higher level officials. It includes representatives of 10 umbrella organizations, business and trade unions, as well as chancellors (the highest state officials in Estonia) of the ministries of Finance, Social Affairs, Education, Culture, and Economic Affairs, and the deputy-chancellor of the Ministry of Interior. The Minister of Regional Affairs chairs the Committee. In addition, a representative of the Estonian Parliament and two government foundations (Enterprise Estonia and Non-Estonians' Integration Foundation) also sit on this Committee.

Further, in June 2006 the *Civic Initiative Support Development Plan*, known as KATA in Estonian, was approved. KATA is one of the results of the Estonian Civil Society Development Concept (EKAK), and it serves to standardize the government's approach to nurturing civil society. Essentially it is a document that brings together information about all the activities from the development plans of the various ministries that are connected with civil society. KATA also aims to replace the activity plan for implementing EKAK as of 2007. The new development plan sets five goals for the next three years: (1) to raise the administrative ability of the public sector in communicating with citizens and NGOs/NPOs; (2) to bring into order the system of financing the NGOs/NPOs; (3) to engage NGOs/NPOs consistently and successfully in the decision-making processes; (4) to raise awareness and develop cooperation between the public, private and the nonprofit sectors and (5) to develop and support civic activism.

NGOs have criticized KATA because they feel that this document does not bring any new ideas. Instead it only reinstates the activities which are already taking place. They feel that KATA failed to provide the qualitative leap in the development of civil society and its cooperation with the Government. For example, as mentioned above, the aim of KATA was to gather information from all ministries' development plans (which are essentially sub-sectoral strategies) on what they are doing in the field of civil society (for example, what does the Ministry for Environment do to support environmental organizations, or the Ministry for Education to support youth and educational NGOs). The main problem however, is that KATA does not perceive civil society as a whole (as EKAK does) but as a sum of specific activities particular to one sector. Therefore, its focus is not on the cross-sectoral issues, e.g., sustainability of NGOs. Further, NGO participation in the development of KATA is also limited, because of the fact that it relies predominantly on the ministries' development plans. To remedy this problem, NGOs are lobbying for the establishment of an implementing unit called the EKAK bureau, which would help the nonprofit sector in taking the ideas and commitments of EKAK forward.

NGO INVOLVEMENT IN POLICY AND DECISION-MAKING PROCESSES

NGO involvement in policy and decision making processes has been understood to include, among others, the possibility and rights for NGOs to have access to information about the process of policy making and law drafting, to be consulted about issues under consideration, and to take active part in defining the process and policy or law in question. Public participation in policy making can be supported through various mechanisms, including: information about the launch of the process, the plans and timelines, sharing early versions of drafts for consultation with NGOs and other stakeholders, including NGOs in working groups which develop the concept of the policy and the draft law from the outset. Participation in decision making processes, on Parliament level, can be realized through allowing NGOs to take part in discussions in Parliamentary Committees or developing reports on the consultation process which would reflect on the input given by NGOs and stakeholders. Opening the processes for participation of NGOs and stakeholders can have many benefits. Primarily, the process can result in fair policies/laws which are reflective of the real needs and are enriched with additional experience and expertise. The participatory process can also facilitate dialogue and consensus on issues, can ensure legitimacy of adopted solutions and guarantee compliance. Participation in the process of developing policies and laws can also increase the feeling of ownership among stakeholders and responsibility for the implementation of the provisions.

The three countries discussed in this article have worked towards analyzing the challenges posed for successful partnership and participation in policy making and integrating the best practice principles into such processes. Out of all three, only Estonia has adopted a Code of Good Engagement which outlines the basic principles of participation while Croatia has initiated a process for drafting such a code.

Hungary

The issue of NGO participation in policy and decision-making processes in Hungary has been a sensitive issue, as governments have not always been open to the involvement of NGOs in such processes. However, the basic principle to enable NGO participation has existed since the change of the political system embodied in the Constitution. Further, there is no one piece of legislation that would detail NGO involvement in policy and decision making processes. Rather, this issue is addressed in various laws and regulations on national or local level.

There is one relevant provision in the Constitution and also in the Act on Legislation, which establish the broad basis for NGOs to participate primarily in the governmental (as opposed to Parliamentary) process on policy-making and law drafting. Although the Act on Legislation contains some specific provisions on NGO involvement, those have not been supported by implementing regulations which leaves them open to various interpretations. In 2005, Hungary made a big step towards public participation when the Parliament adopted the Law of Freedom of Electronic Information, which is the most relevant legislation from the access to information and consultation point of view. This law obliges both national and local governmental bodies to make available on the internet data of public interest. Such data, according to the Protection of Personal Data and the Publicity of Data of Public Interest and also in accordance with some decisions of the Constitutional Court, include not only drafts of laws, but also concepts and other preparatory materials. The law details deadlines, methodology and procedures for publishing such information and reacting on it to give feedback to the public. Further, there are some other mechanisms that depend on Ministry level regulations, such as the various Councils (elderly, youth, social etc.) which also have their own procedures for the involvement of NGOs.

There are also some mechanisms which ensure NGO participation in decision making processes on the Parliament level. The Civil Office (mentioned above) maintains a Parliament "lobby list." NGOs who register on the list are informed and involved in the work of the Parliament. Hungary also adopted a Law on Lobbying in 2006, which caused some controversy. Essentially the law does not apply to NGOs but states that only those entities formally registered under this law may conduct lobbying activities. Therefore, in theory, if the law is interpreted restrictively, it would mean that NGOs are not allowed to lobby in Hungary today. Nevertheless, the practice is different-NGOs are still able to directly contact government officials and MPs about legal reform.

In recent years, NGOs have made successful efforts to influence legislation concerning the sector (e.g. in the case of the National Civil Fund, the Act on Public Interest Volunteering), and more and more results have also been seen in legislation in different fields (such as the environment, disabled rights or women's rights). In addition to cooperation in the legislative process, NGOs and the government have also cooperated with respect to European Union accession issues. The two sectors have also launched partnerships for providing public services (e.g., the Ministries of Health, Social Affairs and Family, Education, and Culture), and they have worked together on processes for determining direct and indirect (delegated) civil representation in European Union institutions. Finally, NGOs also are actively involved in working groups on Ministry levels and they sit on the bodies of the National Civil Fund.

Estonia

In Estonia, consultations with NGOs are mentioned in a governmental decree adopted in 1999 which provides that the explanatory letters of draft laws should also include the opinions of NGOs. In 2005, a *"Code of Good Practice on Involvement"* was developed by representatives of the public sector and NGOs (based on the EKAK), elaborating the key principles that should support active and meaningful participation of NGOs. The Code aims to be applied by administrative agencies in the preparation of at least the following documents: drafts of laws and their amendments; drafts of the regulations and directives of the Government of the Republic; drafts of Ministers' decrees; documents, concepts, policies, development plans, and programs that are important to the country's development; drafts of legislation of European Union institutions and other strategic documents (i.e. green and white books); instruction and procedures for rendering public service; conventions and international agreements, as well as the documents that are worked out within their framework, and that influence the society.

Several studies have shown that civil servants have an increased awareness about the need for civil society involvement. A study conducted in 2006 showed that 92% of civil servants find NGO involvement to be necessary for better results in lawmaking. A more recent qualitative study by Tallinn University showed that civil servants who have permanent contacts with NGOs view the cooperation much more positively, while the lack of experience gives rise to unrealistic expectations, disappointment and prejudice.

The involvement of NGOs in consultations of draft laws and their participation in different working groups and steering committees is increasingly common. The infrastructure of NGOs is well established in Estonia and there are well known umbrella organizations for different sectors in addition to NENO which represents the cross-sectoral advocacy body on behalf of nonprofit sector.

Although NGO participation and consultation is improving, there are still many challenges on the side of both the public and nonprofit sector. The challenges on the side of the public sector are: (1) insufficient knowledge about potential partners (therefore the consultations are often limited for stronger and more known umbrella organizations instead of wider involvement of other types of groups or organizations); (2) insufficient knowledge about the processes of involvement, which makes the consultation process often formal without any real effort to ensure meaningful input from NGOs; (3) poor quality of drafts laws (since they are often very long and complicated texts, that NGOs are not capable to deal with); (4) poor planning of time and short deadlines (The time given to organizations for sending their feedback to draft laws is usually 2-3 weeks, which is often not sufficient when organizations want to gather their members' or constituencies' options first, especially if they are not informed in advance about forthcoming consultation processes. Thus NGOs are often involved only in consultations about ready-made draft laws instead of involving them in the stages of needs assessment and development of the draft); (5) poor capacity in giving feedback to organizations who have contributed to the law-making processes with their proposals.

On the other side, NGOs face the following challenges

(1) lack of resources (both human and financial) to make meaningful contributions to policymaking; (2) lack of competence to comment on legal texts; and (3) lack of ability to consult and involve their members and target groups when they formulate the organization's position towards a policy or law.

The solutions to these problems are being sought through trainings (e.g., NENO's annual summer school in 2007 concentrated on involvement and participation issues, bringing together NGOs and officials to discuss and exchange experiences on how to implement public involvement procedures to achieve the best results) and better funding mechanisms for NGOs (e.g., operational costs for advocacy organizations through the future Endowment).

A further interesting initiative is the new participation portal www.osale.ee ("participate" in Estonian), which was launched by the State Chancellery in summer of 2007. The portal allows civil society groups and individuals to post comments about the ongoing consultation processes, while the ministries can provide the public with draft laws, background materials as well as post polls. In the future, the users will also get the opportunity to initiate legislation and comment on the needs and shortcomings in the society that can currently be done through another portal, "Today I decide." In the first few months the input from public sector has been low, while the feedback from NGOs has been moderate. Nevertheless, the portal has good potential to facilitate the consultation processes.

Croatia

In Croatia, NGO involvement in policy-making and decision making process is still undergoing an initial phase of developing tools and mechanisms for more systematic engagement. Currently, there are no special regulations in Croatia that would guarantee NGO participation at any level of government or parliamentary decision making.

Government's Rules of Procedure prescribe that ministries and other governmental bodies should, when appropriate, forward proposals and opinions to (professional) associations which deal with the issue in the proposal or opinion. However, this provision is not being fully respected and there are no statistics to confirm the efficiency of such an approach. The Parliament's Rules of Procedure provide that "external members of the Parliament 's committees" who are nominated from various expert groups, universities and associations, can give opinions on draft proposals without the voting right. However, only 11 out of 25 different Parliamentary committees can use the option of nominating external members and the procedure of appointment is not transparent.

Due to the lack of systematic involvement of NGOs in the decision-making processes, representatives of NGOs and Government dedicated a special chapter on participation of NGOs in the newly adopted *"National Strategy for Creating Supportive Environment for the Development of Civil Society."* The Strategy indicates the need for the development of unified standards and a mechanism at the national and local level to provide NGOs the opportunity to participate in the drafting, implementation and evaluation of public policies and decisions. Accordingly, the Council for Civil Society Development and Government's Office for NGOs have formed a working group tasked with drafting several possible mechanisms and tools for NGO consultations, such as a Code for NGO Consultations.

Most of the current practice of NGO involvement includes *ad hoc* reactions through the media pressure, advocacy coalitions and direct lobbying after the certain draft proposal (policy or law) has been published. The consequences of this approach are firstly, a significantly low level of access to information about the drafting process (usually conducted in the national or local Government's body) followed by the late publication of the drafts, and secondly, the need for a quick and targeted reaction of NGOs, which does not allow for elaborate comparative analysis or public discussions.

Some NGOs have already established a database of comparative research relating to their main focus of interest and are able to react quickly and produce policy analysis in very short time.

In addition, the process of decision-making, especially on the parliamentary level, is still based on a daily schedule which is constantly subject to change. There is no systematic approach to setting the agenda and thus NGOs face limited possibility and time to prepare meaningfully for the discussions. Moreover, over 80% of legislative drafts are being adopted under so-called "urgent procedures," which in theory should be used only in limited situations. This practice limits the ability of NGOs to participate in decision-making processes.

A more systematic approach to NGO involvement is rare but successful on both the national and local levels. Usually this includes forming a working group for a draft law or policy; the working group is initiated by a governmental body but also includes members of NGOs. Frequent meetings and open discussion and inputs of

NGO members helped bridge the gap between drafting and implementation of certain laws and policies. However, these examples depend on the personal motives and openness of each governmental office.

The main body established by the Government that represents NGOs is the Council for Civil Society Development (described above). In addition to the Council, 53 NGO representatives and experts from the academic sector are involved in the negotiations of Croatian accession to the European Union. Moreover, the Government initiated the establishment of a Joint Consultation's Committee between European Economic and Social Council and Croatia, with two participants nominated by the NGOs participating in its work. Finally, in late 2007, the Government initiated the establishment of the National Council for Promotion of Voluntarism which will include representatives of NGOs.

CONCLUSION

Cooperation between governments and NGOs in the three countries analysed in this article has taken many creative forms. In all three countries, the governments have adopted the basic framework laws which would enable NGOs to operate and sustain their activities. With the exception of the Croatian Law on Foundations and Funds, all of them reflect good practice principles. The tax laws also follow this trend and all three countries have introduced exemptions on income tax and tax benefits for donors which would motivate NGOs to generate their own income and turn to their local communities to gain financial support for their activities. In addition, the volunteering laws in Hungary and Croatia, and the development plan in Estonia aim to create a supportive environment for citizen engagement in the activities of NGOs and social life.

Governments and NGOs have also been innovative in developing mechanisms to improve the financial viability of the sector, especially to address the most common challenge of lack of funding for NGOs' institutional costs. The models described in this article show that there are many creative ways in which governments and NGOs can try to address this problem if they make an assessment of the local needs and opportunities. Each model depends on a distinct source of funding (lotteries, percentage mechanism).

Importantly, the state bodies and NGOs have been able to explore different avenues to increase dialogue and cooperation. They have set up central offices at governmental and parliamentary levels, which are responsible for liaising with NGOs, soliciting their input, working jointly on initiatives of common interest and ensuring their participation in the policy and decision-making processes. The establishment of different departments at ministries tasked to liaise with NGOs ensures that the cooperation is not limited to only one public body but is decentralized and allows for direct partnerships on issues which are close to the parties involved. The programs for cooperation or strategies for support of the development of the sector are important as they embrace and endorse principles and commitments which guide the cooperation and ensure that the support is targeting real needs. The highly participatory processes in the development of these documents are perhaps even more significant as they have brought the public bodies, state authorities and NGOs closer together, have facilitated consensus-building on the priority issues and have created ownership and trust that increase the chances of successful implementation. Finally, the initiatives to translate the principles and rules of NGO involvement in policy-and decision-making processes into codes or regulations have elevated the importance of NGO participation and ensured that all public authorities and NGOs are familiar with the benefits of such involvement and also the obligations and opportunities that arise from it.

The Croatian, Estonian and Hungarian models of cooperation have faced several implementation challenges. The experiences gained through these innovative initiatives have served and can continue to serve as valuable examples and inspiration to other countries that are considering adopting similar approaches in their local environments.

4

Monitoring, Advocacy and NGOs

For many years the term "NGO", usually in its shortened acronym, rather than the full "non-government organisation", was the only term used to describe those organisations outside the government and business worlds, which were involved in development. It was often used to mean only international relief and development organisations. In many places, however, people were unhappy with the idea that such positive organisations defined themselves negatively – by what they were not ("not a government organisation") rather than by what they were ("pro-poor independent voluntary development organisations").

In the nineties with the collapse of the Soviet Union new thinking was coming out of the organisations like Solidarinosc in Poland and Eko-Forum in Bulgaria that rejected the inclusive single party political structure of the Soviet Union and that defined themselves as being organisations separate from the State. They called themselves "civil society organisations" or CSOs. They were a product of the citizens, of "civil society", and distinguished themselves by having a different perspective to the government.

A period of confusion ensued, as the terms NGOs and CSOs were used interchangeably – and this has carried on to the present. Many other terms were also used that added to the confusion: these reflected the particular thinking or particular usage of different countries. Such terms are "Charities", "Private Voluntary Organisations", "Voluntary Organisations", "People's Organisations", "Non-state Actors" and many others. Basically they were all describing the growing number of organisations that are neither from government nor from business, and that are engaged in relief and development, and other public interest issues."

"NGO" has, however, remained in common use, although it has been more clearly defined. There is now general consensus that NGOs are, strictly, a sub-set of Civil Society Organisations and the term describes those formal non-profit and non-government organisations that have a developmental or good governance purpose and that seek funds from one set of actors (usually different from the organisation itself) to apply to the problems of another set of actors (again different from the organisation itself). NGOs are usually defined as organisations that work in the public interest, as defined by the NGO itself. The most up to date definition comes from the Cardoso Report of the UN on the relations between the UN and Civil Society. Many organisations that call themselves NGOs, or are called NGOs by others, have not thought through who they are. They may be embryo political parties, contractors to aid agencies, university think tanks, or people's movements – and may inhabit many other places on this spectrum. Depending on who they are, they may be more or less research oriented, more or less service oriented, or more or less politically oriented. When they are working in the highly sensitive and polarized world of fighting corruption, they need to be clear who they are and what their incentives to action are. An NGO willing to expose corrupt politicians is essentially different from an NGO supplying condoms and safe sex education, or fertilizer, or drinking water. It is useful to follow through the evolution of NGOs that are now working on anti-corruption issues. In many cases they have evolved from NGOs working on elections and democracy issues and who have now become concerned with good governance. They can and should be independent of government, but in some cases they have worked out a collaborative relationship with governments.

Three Sectors in the State

In order to understand the term "civil society" we need to start from a perspective that looks at the State as consisting of three parts-the Government, the Market, and the Citizenry. There have been very many different ways of expressing this-perhaps the most famous being Marc Nerfin's symbolism of the Prince, the Merchant and the Citizen. However we picture the three sections, we still need to clarify what each of them mean and how they differ from each other. If we do this we will be able to identify what is special about the citizen sector (which is synonymous with "civil society"), and then identify what is special about NGOs-which are just one part of civil society, and finally what is special about NGOs that are fighting corruption.

The first sector of the State is the Government Sector (also called the Public Sector): the purpose of this sector is to rule and to govern, and it uses the resources of state property, laws and taxes to enable it to do so. The government also controls the use of force. The Public Sector mobilizes its resources through the power of the law, by coercion and threat, and by command. If, for example, you do not pay your taxes, you are liable to go to prison and the government has the power to make that happen.

The second part of the State is the Business Sector (also called the private sector, the market, or the private non-profit sector): the purpose of this sector is to make profits from returns on invested capital through manufacture, trade and exchange, and they mobilize their resources through the control of private property. A business sees the possibilities for income from providing a good or service that people want, and mobilizes the resources, often from banks, that enable this to happen.

The third part of the State is the Citizens Sector (also called the Third Sector, the Voluntary Sector, or Civil Society). For some people it is just the residual sector left behind after you have deducted the power of the government and the market, but for others the sector has strong positive purposes of its own. The purposes of the Third Sector or Civil Society are:

- to hold the Government Sector and the Business Sector accountable to the citizens
- to enable citizens to associate to advance their common interests
- to improve the lives of the citizens.

The resources of this sector are the citizens' own time, own energy and own personal resources, or the time, energy and resources that they can persuade other people to gift to them. The way that they mobilize these resources is through having shared values with other citizens, and through having a shared commitment to action with includes the family.

In general, however, this diagram is useful because it illustrates:

- The three sectors are of different sizes
- Civil Society is often the smallest in terms of the resources it controls
- The boundaries are fuzzy
- The boundaries between all three sectors overlap.

We must also be aware of pretender organisations that claim social value, but which in reality are organisations formed for personal income, or formed to represent the interests of business or the government or political parties. Because there are increasing numbers of such organisations, and because they are sometimes very clever at disguising themselves, and because civil society NGOs will often be accused of being this kind of organisation, it is important for NGOs to be aware of them. Alan Fowler's book "Striking a Balance" provides a witty and exhaustive of such "pretenders", like GONGOs, (Government owned NGOs), MANGOs (Mafia owned NGOs), and MONGOs (My own NGO).

There are a tremendous variety of civil society organisations, from those that are very formal (e.g. The Red Cross/Red Crescent Organisations) through to those that are very local and very specific to a particular country or group (e.g. burial societies amongst Amharas in Ethiopia, savings and credit associations amongst the Javanese of Indonesia and many West African societies, and age cohorts amongst the Masai in Kenya and Tanzania, and the Nuer in South Sudan). In each case they may be formal to their own members, though not formally established in law. The range is immense: many thousands have come into existence since the collapse of the Soviet Union, and the fall of one-party states: The magazine "Foreign Affairs" in 1996 talked of the "explosion" of civil society organisations. Some may be more inclined to take an interest in anti-corruption issues than others.

SPECIFIC CHARACTERISTICS OF NGOS

NGOs, positioned inside Public Benefit Organizations, have singular governance and programmatic characteristics, and singular constraints that we need to examine. NGOs, which work to fight corruption, are very likely to be attacked on these issues and many people who work for NGOs have not thought these through.

Governance

- NGOs are not for profit; therefore they cannot distribute any surplus they generate as profit to owners or staff. Staff salaries are, however, part of running costs, not surpluses.
- NGOs result from a group of citizens' self-chosen and voluntary initiative to pursue a shared interest or concern – they are not a statutory body, and owe no allegiance to the State
- They govern themselves within whatever legislation they choose to register themselves
- They are formally instituted and accept that they are accountable to the aims and objectives of their originating documents and governing structures.

Many organisations can be set up to meet these

characteristics – this says nothing about what such an organisation actually does. A football fan club, a university, or a paramilitary group could all come under these characteristics. Our definition of an NGO is not complete before we agree on their programmatic activities and values:

Programs

- They exist because certain citizens have identified poverty and injustice as being illegitimate activities that need to be combated. These beliefs are often underpinned by national constitutions or by international conventions and agreements. They may also be underpinned by religious or ideological beliefs.
- They act as intermediary organizations between those who support their work and those they directly target, and have the fiduciary responsibility to their donors to spend the funds that they attract on the programs that they have proclaimed.
- They can work in different ways-through directly providing services to their target group, or through acting variously as a network, a federation of other NGOs, a research organization, or an advocate on behalf of the target group they have identified.

In countries emerging from two or three generations of communism or a one-party state, the genus "NGO" as an independent expression of citizens' interests did not exist-all such ideas of citizens organisations were subsumed within the state or the ruling party e.g. Russia's "Konsomol" and Malawi's "Young Pioneers". Not surprisingly, therefore, there has been no clear model for them of what an indigenous citizens' organisation might look like, and how it might be managed. Into this vacuum has come the western donors' model of an NGO. In some cases this has suggested an independent voluntary organisation with its own mission: but in many cases this has resulted in an aid dependent donor contractor without any local accountability. This is what the aid machine was (and is) prepared to fund, and it is based on the kinds of independent citizens organisations with which western donors are familiar back in their own country. Many NGOs have only come into being since donor funds were being offered for civil society. For many donors the promotion and funding of civil society organisations was seen as a way of supporting democracy and democratic values.

It is not surprising that entrepreneurial individuals who had no knowledge of organisational alternatives to this western model of NGOs, accepted that this was how citizens' organisations did business, and put themselves forward as "NGOs" to take on some of that business. If money were being given out to this new creature called "NGO", then a smart person would become an NGO. Other models of citizen's organisations, like for instance, indigenous cultural organisations, mass movements, or people's associations, did not fit the globalization model and so languished without attention from donors.

Such indigenous forms of organisation, however, have patterns of indigenous communication, accountability and philanthropy that are very valuable for NGOs. If they are not recognized or valued or taken on board, local NGOs will be the poorer. In Bulgaria, as an example, all modern sector NGOs are aid dependent: all old style organs of the previous communist party are reliant on government funding which is now mostly unavailable. One of the few people's organisations that continue with popular support and its own assets is chitalishte (literally: reading room), an adult education association that is present throughout the country, and could, in theory, be a vehicle for all kinds of reformist activities. Examples like this can be found in many countries.

It is true to say that the "NGO" is the model of civil society organisation that has attracted the most attention from foreign donors, and, as a result, has become the dominant model of CSO. There are good and bad NGOs, but the kind that we are promoting in this book have the following characteristics:

- They exist because citizens of the country have a shared belief in the value of certain causes, and have a shared commitment to action in order to reform or improve the problems they have identified. They should not exist simply because donors are prepared to give them funds to do something on the donors' agenda.
- They have the support of citizens in the country who are prepared to back their work with political, financial or human resources. They should not exist only because they have the support of donors. Part of their work is likely to consist in educating citizens about a particular cause so that they can build up the support of the citizens
- They are prepared to take funding from different sources against a clear statement of what they intend such funding to be used for and a commitment to that. They should not use funding offered for one program on another without getting the donors consent – and this donor could be a local

citizen or form just as much as a foreign aid organisation.

- They are prepared to be evaluated as to whether their work has had the results intended, and to be held accountable for those results. They are not simply in existence to carry out activities without ascertaining their impact.
- They are prepared to work within the laws of their country. They are not prepared to use violence in support of their missions, and indeed reject its use.

The reader, from an existing or intended NGO, who intends to be part of the fight against corruption, needs to check their organisation against these characteristics and see how their organisation can be distinguished from, for example, guerrilla movements, political parties, and the mafia.

CHARACTERISTICS OF NGOS THAT FIGHT CORRUPTION

A sober characterization of NGOs that fight corruption at the start of the twenty first century might be as follows:

- Largely dependent on funding from foreign donor organisations that usually comes in restrictive 2-3 year project packages, and leaves the local organisation open to accusations that is merely a pawn of foreign interests
- Largely driven by young politically active people who have "graduated" to anti-corruption work from political reform work and election monitoring
- Largely inspired by public interest concerns against immoral, unethical and harmful behaviour, rather

than simply economic considerations of restrictive practices

- Largely assuming that the citizenry as a whole support their work.

Not surprisingly NGOs that fight corruption will operate differently in different countries. In some countries the task is one of cleaning up exceptions to a generally uncorrupted regime and society: in others, NGOs have to operate within environments of endemic, systematic and structural corruption where it is the rule and integrity the exception – and where political leaders are the ones who head the corrupt practices.

INSTRUMENT TO FIGHT CORRUPTION

The biggest limitation of NGOs as they enter the arena to fight corruption is their self-perception that they are fighting with the backing of the citizenry as a whole, and that this gives them their legitimacy. The way that many are set up, however, does not reflect this position, since they have not historically pursued strategies to increase citizens' backing of their work.

The NGO is usually convinced of the rightness of its cause (and may well underpin those convictions with reference to laws and international conventions), but the NGO usually reflects the opinions of a group of self-selected individuals who have a mission that they have constructed. Most NGOs do not start from a populist platform, and do not have large memberships that provide their constituency. To get popular support they have to convince the citizenry of the rightness of their position, and many NGOs do not spend as much time as they might on such work.

This is a general comment that is by no means true overall. In some cases the main anti-corruption activities from civil society have sprung from activist citizens' organisations that are populist, have a large membership base, and are very effective.

Possible Corruption in NGOs themselves

A fundamentally serious issue in considering the contribution that NGOs can make to fighting corruption is the issue of whether they, themselves, are clean. As we have said earlier, public approval and support of NGOs is often given because they are the seen as a clean alternative to endemic corruption. If NGOs are seen to be just another kind of compromised organisation, this will be very destructive of the public's support for them.

There are two types of corrupt NGOs: the first are knowingly corrupt and are motivated purely by the chance of extracting extra income from donor organisations that they can con. This kind exists wherever there are NGOs and is not so difficult to identify. Those who lead such NGOs are primarily interested in their personal income. What is important is for the NGOs as a whole (or working through a representative organisation) to police their sector, and make sure that such NGOs are exposed where possible, and the reputation of the rest upheld.

The second kind is more difficult to detect and perhaps more insidious. They are the NGOs that practice corruption – particularly with foreign funding – but from good motives. These motives are to support their organizations in the face of that destructive feature of bilateral funding well-known to all who work with it – namely short-term project funding. Short-term project funding together with the onerous conditions that go with it, does not allow an organization to pay its overheads, train its staff, and generally to develop the organization for the long term. It only enables an organisation to manage a short duration project often suggested by a donor, and be, in fact, a donor contractor.

Such NGOs will often "cook the books" – will cut money from over-budgeted salaries, will over-invoice, will change the use of budget lines, will double fund-in order to keep their organization alive and prosperous. The problems come when such behaviour, undertaken for the best of reasons, becomes common practice. It should not be forgotten that such activities often happen in a country where the NGO is surrounded by a culture of corruption in which extortion and bribery to benefit the individual is not only commonly accepted, but hardly ever punished. It becomes a slippery slope for individual NGO staff people to carry out corrupt practices to benefit their organization, and yet to avoid benefiting themselves. Not enough NGOs are aware of the dangers of "benevolent" corruption, and the difficult moral choices it gives its staff.

NGOs that intend to work in fighting corruption must take a long and sober look at themselves. If they tolerate any corrupt behaviour then they should not be involved in fighting corruption until they work out their own ethical dilemmas. More pragmatically, they are very likely to be exposed for corrupt behaviour by those who they will be attacking subsequently, and who will be only too delighted to deflect criticism by counter accusations. In countries where corruption is so endemic that no one is likely to be completely clean, enemies of anti-corruption NGOs will be happy to find examples of corrupt behaviour in NGO personnel in order to cause them to lose their credibility.

NGOS MONITORING – WHAT IT IS AND WHAT IT DOES

Monitoring is an activity carried out to find out what is wrong with a certain situation or individual case. The following elements constitute monitoring:

- It is carried out over a long period of time
- It involves collecting or receiving as much data as possible
- It means close observation of the situation, usually through constant or periodic *examination or investigation or documentation of developments*
- Standards or norms are used as reference to determine what is wrong with the *situation*
- Tools or instruments are used in the process of monitoring
- The product of monitoring is usually a report about the situation
- The report embodies as assessment of the situation which provides a basis for *further action*

The importance of monitoring in fighting corruption is that the reality in any corrupt situation is frequently obscured and concealed-secrecy and concealment are of the essence. Someone therefore has to work to try and pry open the door, look through the window, and bring the antiseptic light of day to what is intentionally hidden and covered up. That person or organisation can be carrying out monitoring.

In some cases what is hidden is hidden intentionally and steps are taken to try and avoid exposure – but in other cases it may simply be that the long established processes (of bureaucracy, for instance) have made people indifferent or unobservant about what is actually happening – or the scale of what is actually happening. Protection rackets by criminal gangs for which police protection is obtained by pay-offs may seem very small when applied to an individual business, but when the scale of such individual payments is monitored, and when the impact of such payments on police behaviour is analysed, ordinary people may be shocked at the way small "contributions" may be fuelling a large and complex corrupt police system. The Kenyans call corruption "kidogo" ("a little thing") although everyone knows that it can range from little to very big.

Monitoring is, by definition, a long-term, if not permanent, performance review process. However, shorter-term efforts using the same approach can also be valuable in obtaining a "snapshot" picture of a given situation. A repetition of such observations would be necessary in order to measure progress over time, i.e. to find out whether the indicators captured in the "snap shot" were improving or worsening. A sequence of snapshots will be able to show evidence of changes over time, but methodologically, the snapshots must be comparable.

NGO MONITORING

Monitoring related to government corruption can and should be conducted through government itself in those countries where there is political will to fight corruption and in which there are official monitoring agencies that can be trusted. Thus independent agencies of the government, like a Supreme Audit authority, or an Ombudsman's office, or a specific Anti-Corruption Commission (or other "watchdog" agency) can be competent monitors of corruption and allies for NGOs in monitoring corrupt practices. At an inter-governmental level, agencies of the European Union and the Council of Europe also carry out monitoring of government corruption on behalf of their multinational constituencies.

But, as in a number of other areas, there are powerful reasons why monitoring by governments and international institutions alone is insufficient. Governments have inherent incentives to distort the results of their monitoring of corruption and anti-corruption activities if such monitoring is going to expose things they want to keep hidden. Apart from the incentives that individual government officials have to keep things hidden, evidence of high levels of corruption is a potential vote loser, and thus not relished by any government that wants to stay in power.

It is also possible that international organisations, particularly bilateral organisations, have strong strategic reasons not to expose the problems of countries that, for other reasons, are their allies. It is not likely to be in the interests of those supporting Palestinian nationhood, for instance, to have the extent of the corruption in the Palestinian state to be exposed. International monitoring efforts, however, are likely to be limited in scope and resources, and have incomplete access to the local level. They are unlikely to research in as much depth as a national or local NGO.

For all the above reasons, anti-corruption monitoring is an important activity for NGOs. It was stated earlier in this chapter that one of the purposes of NGOs was to hold the Government and Business sectors accountable to the citizens. Monitoring is an important part of this watchdog role, and NGOs are likely to be able to have a considerable amount of access to local knowledge, local experience, and local contacts.

From the NGO perspective, monitoring has been defined as: *Monitoring is a broad term, used in many contexts, that describes various stages of collection, verification, and analysis by NGOs of information concerning public interest issues, including civil, political, social and economic rights.*

A great number of NGOs in many societies around the globe monitor the work of public and private institutions in their country to protect the public in a number of different areas they consider important – elections, land appropriation, gender representation – and many others. Such monitoring will also vary from merely keeping themselves informed through to a systematic information collection structure. The exact objective of each monitoring effort is likely to be different, but it is important to be clear at the outset. Objectives might be, for instance:

- To monitoring the observance by public officials or other entities (e.g. political parties) of their duties under anti-corruption statutes, for example asset declaration provisions.
- To ascertain levels and causes of corruption in a specific institution or area on a systematic basis with the objective of providing useful information that can be helpful for the formulation of policies. This may take the form of identifying areas where NGOs can suggest improvements need to be made, or assisting governments in carrying out their own anti-corruption policies through independent verification that those policies have indeed been implemented.

- Muckraking – to describe and draw public attention to important examples of corruption or related phenomena, in order to generate public pressure for certain policies or against certain practices.

NGO monitoring work will greatly depend upon whether the government has adopted and publicly embraced an anti-corruption program. If they have, then the role of independent civil society organisations vis-à-vis monitoring will be to:

- Monitor that the existing corruption plan is actually being implemented as it was planned
- Point out publicly or specifically to the government the shortcomings in its implementation and their effect on limiting corruption

If, on the other hand, there is no government plan, and little political leadership for limiting corruption, then the primary job of the NGO is to:

- To point out forcefully to the government and the public the damaging effects of corruption and the need for an anti-corruption plan and activities
- To identify principal systems or processes vulnerable to corruption, and to propose actions and reforms that could be taken to reduce opportunities for corruption
- To research and monitor corrupt acts and the effects of corrupt acts and keep bringing these to the public and the government's attention
- To build coalitions for action to limit corruption, based upon and involving future monitoring activities.

Monitoring is, before everything else, a factual and

objective process: when this is done by an NGO then that NGO's credibility will depend on the competence and professionalism that it shows in the implementation of its activities, and the quality of the information it gathers and publishes. Where and when the NGO is credible this allows individuals, groups or organizations from various backgrounds in the country to initiate discussions and develop a debate using as a common basis the information gathered by the NGO. When the NGO is not credible, this will soon be revealed, and will render useless the debate the NGO hoped to engender, and the subsequent pressure for change.

We have said that monitoring is a "factual and objective" process: objectivity does not mean an absence of emotional commitment to an issue. The NGO is likely to be motivated by a strong ethical desire to improve an unacceptable situation, and, when it is doing its monitoring work, it should be proactive in seeking the truth, investigating issues, looking for data and exposing facts about corruption. Monitoring, however, should be fair and even-handed, and this means equal treatment for all participants – until they condemn themselves. An NGO setting out to monitor a particular issue should not pre-judge that it is going to find out a particular quantity of corruption – but should have confidence in the methods that it used will reveal the truth. The NGO should not be selective about the information it is trying to uncover and it should expose all information that it finds, whether it highlights corruption or the absence of corruption.

Besides adding to the monitor's credibility, if the monitoring NGO discovers good practice, then there is value in mentioning this as it may encourage less corrupt officials to cooperate with the monitoring project.

Monitoring projects and their findings can therefore be a positive effort to reward good practice, as well as an effort that exposes bad practice. The tool of monitoring can be used as both the carrot and the stick to promote change.

The Targets of Monitoring

When an NGO decides to monitor corruption, the target for the monitoring can be a wide range of institutions and individuals, including:

- Governments-Ministries, Ministerial departments, official representatives, staff (from national and central to local levels)
- The Private Sector-private sector associations, private companies, employees and representatives
- Financial institutions – responsible individuals, and employees
- Political parties – individual politicians, and staff of political parties
- Parliament-individual members of parliament and those responsible for Parliament, at both national and local levels
- The Judiciary – judges, lawyers, those employed by the courts

Specific points for observation by the monitoring NGO should then be tailored to each of the groups or individuals who will be monitored. Indonesian Corruption Watch, for instance, in its effort to track corruption in the courts, spent considerable time sitting outside the courts watching who went in and out of the court buildings, and cultivating friendships with the clerks of court. From this they were able to deduce who introduced who to whom for the purposes of corrupt payments to judges – since they had earlier ascertained that the judges themselves did not take money directly from those intending to bribe them.

Corruption may seem a difficult subject to monitor, given that those involved usually spend a great deal of effort attempting to conceal it. It therefore makes sense for NGOs attempting to monitor corruption to be proactive in thinking where corruption is likely to take place, or where there are opportunities for corruption, and monitor them as well. If the target knows that he or she is being monitored, then he or she may attempt to conceal information, and this itself may be something worth monitoring and revealing. Documenting the attempts to conceal information from the NGO monitor may then become an important part of the monitoring project.

Monitoring can be a simple exercise requiring few resources (perhaps one person watching what happens in a key location), as well as a complex venture that can be very costly, involving a large number of researchers trying to get access to information in a large number of places. Choosing which areas are to be the subject for monitoring must be done with care, and there are a number of possibilities about what can be strategically chosen for monitoring with an aim of getting the key information that will reveal the truth about what is happening.

The Philippines Centre for Investigative Journalism, for instance, wanted to document President Estrada's corruption. What they decided to do was to track down the house ownership certificates for the houses that President Estrada had bought for his numerous mistresses as a way of proving that he was spending money way beyond what he had access to as a President of the Philippines. In trying to get information about illegal logging it chose to monitor: "exploitation without title, exploitation out of boundaries, exceeding period of exploitation granted, exploitation of unauthorised species, no demarcation of boundaries and no marking of logs".

The NGO may also notice a procedure not being followed, for example the full declaration of assets by a senior government official in a country where there is an asset disclosure program. The NGO then needs to look in detail at the steps and timeline of the official procedure as set down by the administration, by the law and by available official documentation. Against this identified set of norms, the NGO may be able to monitor flaws in implementation of this procedure (e.g. swift transfers of assets to family members before disclosure). This can be a relatively simple monitoring action.

Key Activities in Monitoring

In the examples given above monitoring implies going to different locations and documenting what is happening or collecting testimony to determine what has already happened. Taking pictures or video footage, collecting documents, recording locations and identifying processes are all part of this process. There is also the kind of monitoring which is purely office based, such as monitoring the media, checking publicly available financial reports, or records of ownership, checking fund-raising information, and analyzing public records of private companies.

There is also considerable logistical work to be done-preparing questionnaires, managing data in the different forms of documents, videos, photographs, databases of names and events, and maybe data on location coordinates for mapping purposes. Data analysis will have to be undertaken and a report written, published and distributed as frequently and regularly as the project plan requires them. Each key activity forms part of a chain and if a link is weak or not dependable then the whole project may fail.

All these activities will enable the NGO doing the monitoring (or some other organisation) to put reliable information in front of people with the power to make decisions that can change the situation for the better-if there is the political will to do so. Where there is not the political will, the same information may used to generate it, by exposing such information to the public, international organisations and others-and showing the shortcomings of the official response.

Corruption often takes place where processes are opaque to public scrutiny and there may be many different kinds of people who are trying to acquire the same information, trying to conceal it, or trying to put some "spin" on it so that it is understood differently. There may be sizeable discrepancies between what is actually happening, statements by government officials about what they say is happening, and information from other organisations or individuals who may have little or no field experience of fighting corruption. This will be compounded by the different stakeholders having different levels of seriousness or commitment about eradicating corruption. To one person a bribe to a policeman may be considered a small thing, and part of the tribulations of everyday life. To another it is a small cog in a large off-budget corrupt financing machine of the police. NGOs have to very careful to report what is actually happening, and to do this in ways that can be checked to ensure their credibility. They must be ready to defend their findings, and avoid getting caught up in "spin". Testing the Rhetoric and Finding where the Real Problem is Monitoring tests the rhetoric against the reality in a situation of potential corruption by verifying the actual implementation of processes against what people say is happening, and providing the evidence of the lack of action and the consequences of this-if such is indeed the case. The NGO can verify lack of action through carrying out a monitoring activity that can provide stakeholders with hard evidence of where processes do not function. An analysis can then be undertaken to identify if the lack of action is due to lack of will, to lack of means or institutional shortages or to intentional corruption. The following may be the problems:

- Lack of implementation of stated commitments
- Lack of or biased law enforcement
- Lack of transparency
- Non cooperation of individuals or government departments
- Flaws, contradictions or shortages in legislation
- Lack of appropriate funding mechanisms
- Lack of appropriate staffing
- Lack of technical knowledge or equipment.

Institutional shortages are often advanced as excuses for the problems listed above, but this can be special pleading to cover up problems related to obstruction or corruption. A Ministry may say that it does not have the staff to check on corrupt practices as an excuse for the continuation of corrupt practices, but the real situation is a lack of willingness to change and an entrenched attitude of impunity. An example of this is seen in the Case Study of Civil Monitoring of Presidential Decree No.

95 in Georgia. The presidential decree was a strong statement by the President of Georgia against corruption. The coalition of Georgian NGOs which monitored the implementation of the anti-corruption decree concluded, however, that "the Government of Georgia lacked the political will to fully implement the decree and combat the existing widespread corruption. The project was an important contribution to the subsequent political change in Georgia in November 2003". Clarifying the actual situation made it easier to expose the reality behind the rhetoric.

The identification of lack of action to develop working anti-corruption measures in a reasonable time can well be seen (and published) as an indicator of corruption itself. This can provide a powerful tool to rethink the main excuses put forward by the subject accused of corruption.

We should also accept that, sometimes, the subject agrees on the need for implementing the measures identified as "best practice" but really does lack financial, human or technical resources to implement them. Under those circumstances, monitoring exercises can point out the need for targeted technical assistance programmes, which have a chance of being effective, providing the commitment to reform corruption is there.

MONITORING INVESTIGATES THE FUNCTIONING OF SYSTEMS

Government policy, ministerial regulations and established procedures are intended to lead to a set of desired outcomes: three examples from the construction sector illustrate this:

- A poverty eradication policy sets the framework to lift the poorest to a higher quality of life through a number of proposed actions, including improvement to their housing.
- Building regulations are intended to lead to good housing development, sewerage disposal systems, and safe roads.
- Procedures for the allocation of construction contracts are there to make sure the government receives value for money and employs companies qualified to undertake the housing work. Monitoring at the policy level can gauge the effectiveness of policy implementation. In developed as well as developing countries, stated policy aims are simply not met. Monitoring can help to:
- Determine if any actions to support policy implementation are actually being taken
- Determine if actions taken are effective at delivering the policy objectives or not
- Where actions are ineffective, promote the development of more effective actions to implement the policy objectives
- Highlight the need for funding or other resources to tackle the problems

Monitoring at the regulatory level can help establish whether indeed good housing, sewerage and roads have resulted: whether the poor have a higher quality of life, and whether the government gets value for money

- Whether building regulations have been observed
- If they have not, whether illegal activities are being investigated

- Whether identified illegal activities are being prosecuted
- Whether penalties are being enforced, and lastly, whether the penalties imposed are, in fact, a deterrent.

Monitoring at the procedural level can gauge whether the processes to identify the best builders were carried out, and whether the government is getting value for money

- Whether proper tendering procedures were carried out
- Whether contracts were properly awarded on the basis of those tendering procedures.

Monitoring is also a tool that is able to highlight systematically over time where systems do not work, and thus allow for corrupt practices to take place. Such highlighting is often a precursor and base for advocacy action to take place subsequently.

If an NGO knows, for instance, that the Police are demanding and getting illegal fees over and above the official fees for vehicle licensing, the NGO can set up a simple form implemented covertly for recording the official rates, the actual fees paid, the dates, and if possible the payers. It the NGO uses that information to make a fuss about such illegal payments, and the Police commit to reforms, the NGO can go back later to see if the payments are still being made. The NGO can also calculate the amount of illegal income that the Police are gathering each day, or other agreed period, and use this information as a tool to demand reforms, and create an advocacy campaign around this issue. Monitoring is a Tool that Needs Access to Information

Monitoring needs to establish a baseline or standard, and then needs data to compare against that baseline. For these reasons it requires access to information to the greatest extent possible at all levels relevant to the issue. The obvious place to look for information is in the media – particularly the press. In some countries there is a strong tradition of freedom of the press, and the press are responsible and professional. In other countries the media is owned and controlled by people who may be part of the corruption problem, and will be unhappy at allowing their papers or TV channels to report such information. In such cases, an NGO fighting corruption needs to go beyond the existing media and look for other information that is publicly available.

"Publicly available" is a term that is capable of a lot of interpretation in many countries. Only a few countries have put into place a Freedom of Information Act (FOI), and the existence of the Act may mask a large number of difficulties in actually using its provisions. To give general information to the reader about FOIs, and to act as a pointer for the future (since monitoring NGOs may well get involved in the promotion of an FOI law), an article on Freedom of Information laws.

If an NGO thinks it is necessary to use the provisions of FOI laws, they should be carefully studied in advance to assess what is necessary to file a successful application for information. The framework that exists for enforcing FOI provisions should also be carefully studied to make a realistic assessment of the chances of success.

South Africa has an Access to Information Act, but, as we see from the PSAM-Public Service Accountability Monitor, it is not always easy to get the information. They say: "Once a Promotion of Access to Information Act request is made, departments have, according to the terms of the act, 30 days to respond to PSAM. Failure to do so is considered a refusal, according to the terms of the Act. This refusal is then appealed by PAM and, again according to the terms of the Act, a further 30 day period is given to the department to respond to the information request. If this period also results in non-compliance, the issue is presented to the court".

Where there is a good tradition of investigative journalism, this is a gold mine for an NGO carrying out monitoring. The NGO should make friends with the journalists, and research the back issues of the newspapers that cover applicable investigative stories for the information that it could use. There are world-class organizations like the Centre for Public Integrity with its world network of investigative journalists, and national organizations, like the Philippines Centre for Investigative Journalism that is largely credited with bringing down President Estrada. NGO monitors have to be careful, however, about the competence and professionalism of journalists and media that revel in scandals, and exposes. They may well be partisan, and their work may not be based on good journalistic standards. The downside of using these sources is that information they provide may be based on rumors, or on wrong or biased information.

Given that the monitoring NGO's credibility is absolutely essential to maintain a credible monitoring project, there is no room for error. The Monitoring NGO should draw from these sources, but carry out investigative activities itself (perhaps by hiring in an investigative journalist if they do not have such capacity themselves) to separate rumors from fact, gather additional data or ensure that all documentation provided is useable in court, or is of sufficient quality to support a developing dossier.

Stakeholders

While various stakeholders involved in the issue identified for a monitoring effort may see advantages to a monitoring project being developed, they will not all necessarily have the same reasons for doing so. It is an important task for the NGO doing the monitoring to consider what might be the incentives for different stakeholders. This could to add leverage to its operating framework, to provide opportunities for giving and receiving training in how corruption works (and how it can be combated), and to create avenues for media interest.

Incentives for getting access to strategic information may also help to build alliances with politically powerful institutions and facilitate communication with otherwise ambivalent organisations. Being aware of other stakeholders' motivations and information requirements can help the monitor keep them actively engaged, which may lead to increased information flows for the project and support achievement of the overall project objectives.

The kinds of stakeholders who may find monitoring and its results attractive to them include Government, the Private Sector, and the international donor community for some of the following reasons:

Government

- Government can proudly point out that an independent monitor is looking at their efforts. This adds to their reputation for transparency.
- Government can instantly publicize any progress that is made. While this may not be an instant

resolution of all problems, progress can be seen (and reported) in reasonable time exhibiting the tackling of problems, improvement in procedures, increases in transparency, and increases in the seriousness with which topics are being addressed.

- The NGO can provide recommendations where it notes that a procedure has shortfalls. This can contribute to improved legislation and functioning of government.
- The NGO and government officials may learn from each other while working together. Increased transparency on processes through the monitoring NGO's work can increase external understanding of the functioning of governmental institutions and demystify processes.
- Significant sums of money may be recovered by the government in unpaid taxes or fines, if monitoring identifies such.
- The NGO is not subject to the same pressures as government and may be able to act where individuals in government cannot. At the local level, government officials may have the will to tackle cases of corruption, but face significant pressures from companies, local elites and others involved. The monitor can act as a conduit for those officials, as it would for representatives of civil society.
- The public often has a deep-rooted mistrust of government officials where corruption is a common fact of life. The NGO monitor can change these dynamics through increasing transparency and gradually help trust to be regained.
- Openly and overtly addressing corruption through

agreeing to an NGO monitoring project may improve the image of the country abroad. This can have many benefits including attracting foreign investment from companies wishing to operate in a more stable environment.

The Private Sector

- Corruption can give some companies an unfair comparative advantage. The best of sector companies are then discouraged from investing in countries where corruption prevails. This results in a potential huge financial loss to the government, as worst of sector companies often do not pay the required taxes, deliver poor service and substandard products, avoid regulations etc. Monitoring can reduce this unfair comparative advantage by exposing bad practices and encouraging sanctions to level the playing field or eliminate illegal operators from it.
- Companies that operate in a transparent manner both benefit from a better market image and are unlikely to be adversely affected by corruption monitoring applied by national and international NGOs.
- Companies can use the monitor as a confidential avenue to report corrupt practices by government officials, which can become crippling and restrict their expansion. Companies may face some problems linked to corrupt practices, but be unable to tackle them openly from within because of pressure on their staff by these same government officials. A dialogue can be established with the monitoring NGO that allows them to report on

corrupt practices to a wide audience whilst maintaining anonymity for the sources.

- The Private Sector often comes under attack from international and local NGOs and vice-versa. Frustration can build up on both sides if neither feels they are listened to, leading to a stalemate. The process of documentation by the monitoring NGO is neutral and open to input from all parties. The project objectives, information gathered and conclusions drawn are transparent. Monitoring reports can therefore allow different groups to understand more about each other's constraints as well as each other's progress.

The International Donor Community

- Many projects initiated and supported by international donors fail to deliver expected outputs due to corruption and the embezzlement of funds. The monitoring NGO undertakes a reality check on program implementation using identified indicators of progress. This can support performance-linked donor disbursements set against the completion of concrete milestones.
- Donor funded programs are often poorly implemented and misuse of funds occurs where corruption exists. If the monitoring NGO can get data on fund use that evidences embezzlement this will inform donors on the points of weakness in the administration of many of their programs and improve their efficiency. Should embezzlement and corruption be tackled, it might even be true that special donor funded programs are unnecessary, since the government will have its own resources.

- Increased transparency in a given sector can be used to improve other sectors. Structural Adjustment Programs supported by donors focus on the development of a free market economy which it is recognized can only deliver the intended benefits where social justice and transparency exist. Monitoring provides a direct way of identifying this and thus tackling corruption.
- Donors often have very little information on corrupt practices and how these affect their programmes. In order to assess the impact they often rely on information provided by the same officials who may be participating in corruption. Independent monitoring provides donors with third party, objective and detailed information on governance, loss of revenues, public tensions and program implementation. Monitoring is a tool that is valuable in itself, but is made more effective when joined with public information and advocacy.

Although the monitoring NGO's findings may highlight important discrepancies and de *facto corrupt practices, little action may be taken by key stakeholders on the* monitoring NGO's findings, unless advocacy at various levels promotes it. If the information is not used quickly, then delays in turning the NGO's findings into action reduces their potential impact, and targeted groups may use as an attacking gambit the argument that the information is out of date, and no longer reliable or relevant.

While the NGO may be pushing for greater public information and increased transparency, the publication of findings may be met by a lack of interest. This can be due to:

- High level political pressures discouraging donors from using leverage, which can be very useful to promote local change
- National or international disinterest in the issue
- High financial stakes pressuring stakeholders into maintaining the status-quo
- A slow reaction from stakeholders who may be engaged on other issues
- Poor publication and dissemination of the Monitor's findings

It is important to recognize that pushing for action by 'friendly stakeholders' who committed their support to the monitoring project can require as much planning, strategy and resources as the monitoring itself.

The NGO can document that a system is dysfunctional and suggest changes that need to be made for it to be effective, but it has the limitations when it comes to promoting action:

- If the same NGO agitating for action on an issue, or "advocacy", was previously carrying out the monitoring, some will accuse it of having "cooked" the monitoring in order to lead it to advocacy. The best defense against such accusations is for the monitoring to be objective and professionally sound.
- The NGO may have limited its monitoring to a specific system or time period, and not have enough information to warrant a full scale advocacy campaign. The defense against this is to consider in advance what you are going to monitor and make sure that it is pertinent to a possible future advocacy campaign.

In general, however, monitoring, if well chosen with advocacy in mind, can be the most effective way of gathering information that will subsequently be of great value in educating the public about the particular issue at hand, and contributing to the advocacy campaign that aims to reform that same issue.

NGOS AND ADVOCACY

Not only do NGOs compete for each other's skilled staff, but they also compete for clients, funding, media attention, and favours parcelled out by government officials. This unfortunate situation does not augur well for NGO solidarity. In addition, the culture of participation in China also seems to work against NGO collective action. As explained earlier, the institutional design in China encourages individual actions aimed at persuading bureaucrats to use their discretionary power to the advantage of the parties engaging in those actions. At present the government has no clearly stipulated obligation to support NGOs, therefore they cannot demand any concrete assistance from the government by citing any regulation or policy. Meanwhile, a particular NGO can often obtain some individually negotiated favours from officials or government agencies if it enjoys good relationships with them or is skilled at soliciting their support. Consequently it makes more sense for individual NGOs to quietly cultivate good relationships with government officials in order to obtain particularistic favours than to work together with other NGOs to fight for universal rights and benefit. When a particular NGO has indeed received special favours from government officials, it is usually wise for it to keep it from other NGOs. Under such circumstances, the NGO is also likely to consider its own interests to be better served by forging close ties with the government rather than with other NGOs, and it is less likely to damage its good relations with the government by challenging any government policy or practice.

A few examples can serve to demonstrate this situation. A NGO in Guangzhou managed to get 100,000 yuan from a government fund in 1999. Its manager told some other NGOs about it. Afterwards she was reproached for being ungrateful by officials, who said: 'You should have kept quiet. Why did you have to let everybody know? What can we do if they all come here to ask for money?' In Beijing, grapevine rumours suggest that a couple of NGOs have powerful patrons in the relevant government agencies. Each of them is identified by other NGOs as the protege of a particular government official. Other NGOs all have bitter tales to tell about how the patrons treated them unfairly in order to give advantage to their proteges. One NGO manager went to ask an official, who was said to be an old friend of the manager of her rival organisation, why his agency had given four times more money to the other NGO, which she considered to be poorly managed. She was told that since her organisation was in a stronger position, more money should go to the weaker one.

When NGOs working in the same field feud with each other, it also hinders collective actions by their members or clients. A few years ago, a NGO leader in one of the cities where I have conducted research asked the parents of children who received service from her organisation to take the lead in forming a parents' association in order to promote the rights of mentally disabled people. The plan was to bring together all the parents of mentally disabled children in that city under the association.

However, it was frustrated by the long-standing friction between the NGOs from the very beginning. As the president of the association told me:

> If we call our organisation the association of parents of X city, then we cannot just have parents linked to one organisation. However, since the association was formed at the suggestion of the leader of one NGO, others all identified us with this particular NGO. This rather limited our scope, so we decided that in order to avoid being identified with this NGO we should adopt a detached attitude and place ourselves above the concerns of individual organisations. However, this attitude offended the NGO leader who first proposed the association so she also started to give us the cold shoulder. Since other people were not showing much interest in us and this NGO leader also cold-shouldered us, we were left in an increasingly awkward position. So, after organising a few activities we did not want to carry on any more.

Factionalism was not the only problem which had plagued the parents' association. Government policy on the registration of NGOs was another major obstacle it had encountered in striving to be an effective advocate for the interests of its members. Since the Disabled Persons' Federation, a semi-official organisation, already exists in every city, other organisations which aim to represent the interests of disabled people are unlikely to be allowed to register. In any case, the parents' association could not persuadé any government agency to agree to act as its sponsor, therefore it could not register itself and remained strictly speaking an illegal organisation.

Although the government did not take any action against it, its lack of a legitimate status further dampened the enthusiasm of its members. As the president said:

'Every time we want to organise a meeting or send out a notice to our members, we cannot just go ahead with it. We have to do it through the disabled person's federation. They said to us: 'You are illegal.' So there is a big unresolved problem there for us.'

In another city, some parents of autistic children organised regular activities amongst themselves for years. They called themselves a 'club' although it appeared to be a full-blown formal organisation in every respect. For example, the members elected an executive council once every four years and they paid annual membership fees which were used to publish a newsletter, among other things.

The club organised a wide range of activities, e.g., inviting specialists from other cities to give training and lectures to its members; conducting surveys of the needs of families with autistic children; drawing media attention to the lack of social service for autistic children. In fact, it was the best-organised grassroots autonomous organisation I had ever come across in China. Since 1996, the club had been trying to register as an independent organisation.

Obviously it had not been easy for it to gain approval from the government. When representatives of the club first went to see government officials, they were considered troublemakers and were refused a reception. However, with perseverance and the right tactics the club eventually gained the sympathy of relevant government officials. In 1998, the Civil Affairs Bureau of the city finally decided to allow the club to register. However, before the registration went ahead, the Falun Gong incident took place. Afterwards the registration of new popular organisations was frozen and the club was told by civil affairs officials that no new organisation of its kind would be approved in the next 5 to 10 years.

With the campaign to straighten out social organisations underway after the Falun Gong incident, the members of the club were afraid of carrying on their activities without a legitimate status, therefore the club was left with one choice, i.e., to become the 'subsidiary' of a registered organisation. The city has a semi-official organisation called the Mental Health Association. Its leaders agreed to let the parents' club 'hang under' it. However, there were serious concerns among the parents that once the club became a subsidiary organisation of the Mental Health Association, it would lose its autonomy, and its freedom to organise activities would be restricted. The fear seemed to be well-founded. As one parent related to me:

> Last time we met with the secretary general of the Association he said: 'In the past some parents insisted on remaining independent. They were going too far.' Then I mentioned that we wanted to invite certain experts from other cities to come here to give us some training. The secretary general immediately reacted by saying: 'Once you have joined our association, we will take care of these things. You parents can just sit back and act as our advisers.'

Members of the club split up into two camps: those who favoured affiliation with the Mental Health Association, because this seemed to be the only legitimate means for them to continue working for the interests of autistic children and their families; and those who were against affiliation with the association, thinking that they could only carry out effective advocacy by being an independent organisation. Eventually those parents who favoured affiliation with the association joined it as individual members of its newly-formed Youth and Children Branch. The rest of the parents, a minority, became 'dispersed', and the club ceased operation. The parents who joined the association had hoped that some of them would be allowed to serve on the executive council of the Youth and Children Branch, so that they would have some influence on its decision-making, but it turned out that the association did not reserve a single place on the council for them. When I spoke to a couple of the parents who joined the association four months afterwards, they remained disappointed about the benefit of the new arrangement.

The collapse of the parents' club shows how NGO's advocacy function can be seriously restricted by current government regulations, but there are also other factors which prevent bottom-up NGOs from becoming effective advocates for their members. One major obstacle seems to be the prevalent pessimism (or realism) among ordinary people about what they can achieve with their actions. In my interviews with parent leaders and NGO managers, many of them stressed that NGOs should not set unrealistic goals for themselves and should be sympathetic to the government's position. For example:

When so many able-bodied people have been laid off, how can we realistically expect the government to give subsidies to families with disabled people, or find disabled people jobs? My brother lives in New Zealand. I have heard from him that in New Zealand the government takes care of everything for disabled children. There are special provisions for them so they receive more benefits than normal children. If we want China to do the same, I am not even sure if it can be achieved 50 years from now, so I don't blame the government. There is no point in pressuring it to do what it is incapable of doing.

I have said on various occasions that the economy of our country has not developed to a stage when we can expect the government alone to pay for the care of our disabled children, so let individuals, families, and society all contribute to it. I always say to other parents that we should face the reality and should not shout abuses in public whenever we are dissatisfied with things.

Government officials are not really unsympathetic to our cause, so I have much understanding for them. For example, I ran into a retired director of the Education Bureau and he said to me: 'Don't blame me for refusing to support you in the past. We really did not have enough money. You should have seen the condition of normal schools. When normal schools were still seriously under-funded, where could we find the resources for special education schools?' So I said to him: 'Yes, I understand.'

Even if they are not totally pessimistic about their ability to make a difference, most people want quick solutions to their problems and are impatient to wait for advocacy activities to change government policies or popular attitudes. Most revealing is the remark of a participant at a group discussion during a national conference of parents of mentally disabled children. The remark was made in response to another participant's suggestion that they contact representatives to the People's Congress to ask them to introduce new legislation concerning social service provision for disabled children:

It is too slow a remedy to be of any help. Even if we can make the People's Congress adopt new legislation to provide social services for disabled children, it may take five years for it to happen, but we cannot wait that long.

By then our children will have become grown-ups. So let us focus on practical issues instead.

The scepticism about what can be achieved plus preoccupation with immediate needs make many people reluctant to devote time and energy to any activity which does not promise quick results or concrete benefit to themselves. This is another factor which explains why the association of parents of mentally disabled people mentioned above has not being an effective advocacy organisation. As the president said: 'The Chinese people are very practical. They only make investments when they are assured of returns. If there is going to be a 50% gain, people will give you 50% support, otherwise they give you nothing. Because there was no concrete benefit, parents were not keen on the association.'

In another case, a British couple, both specialists in education and rehabilitation for mentally disabled children, founded an organisation called Guangdong Special Children Parent Club in Guangzhou. The British couple obtained external funding to set up a resource centre for parents of mentally disabled children. The centre employs both administrative and professional staff. The latter provide professional consultation and assessment services for parents. The club's 100 or so members include parents of autistic children as well as parents of children with other types of mental disability, e.g., Down Syndrome and cerebral palsy. Although the club is intended to bring families in similar situations together so that they can join forces in 'improving public perceptions, awareness and attitudes toward children with disabilities', instead of pulling together, it seems that the members of the club have formed informal subgroups which quarrel with each other over the use of the club's resources. The preoccupation with immediate needs as opposed to long-term goals drew parents of children with the same type of disability together. For example, parents of autistic children organised activities specifically targeting autism using the resources of the club. Other parents were disgruntled because they felt those families got more out of the public resources of the club than they did. Parents of autistic children remained unrepentant, saying that the resources of the club were for everybody, so if other parents did not know how to make good use of the resources it was their problem. Meanwhile they also started to organise activities amongst themselves outside the club to avoid squabbles with other parents, which further weakened the sense of unity among members of the club.

5

Building Networks: Community and Government Relations

For the purposes of this reference guide, "community relations" is defined as any interaction among beneficiaries, businesses, and NGOs. The usefulness of your organization and the success of your projects will largely be determined by relations within the community, as the community is where the NGO operates. While carrying out your NGO mission, you will most likely interact with a host of people—political parties, community leaders, business people, potential donors, various NGOs, and your beneficiaries. These entities represent your community.

RELATIONS WITH BENEFICIARIES

The success of your program will largely be determined by the extent to which you include beneficiaries, those individuals your project is designed to help, in the planning process. In order to include them, conduct surveys, focus groups, or other forms of information-gathering to determine the perspectives and opinions of your beneficiaries. You can also invite community leaders or prominent individuals from among your beneficiaries to join in group meetings or periodic monitoring meetings during a project.

Moreover, beneficiaries should play an integral role in implementing your project. To the extent that this is possible, your projects should promote the eventual independence of your beneficiaries. When problems arise during a project, soliciting input from beneficiaries can often lead to the best solution. Most importantly, consider the requests and advice the beneficiaries have to offer when formulating strategies or plans. They know what needs and challenges they have and may offer the best ideas for addressing them.

Challenges

Working with beneficiaries has several challenging aspects. These challenges include difficulties in gaining their trust and resistance to accepting aid.

In all societies, particularly in less politically and economically secure environments, individuals can be distrustful or skeptical of outsiders or foreigners. If NGO members are not native to the community they seek to serve, the community may be naturally distrustful of them. In order to overcome initial mistrust or misunderstanding, your NGO must engage in trust-building activities with the community so as to gain legitimacy and respect.

One way to win trust is to gain an endorsement from a prominent institution or individual in the community. Promoting interactive dialogue among members of the community is another way to enhance understanding and acceptance of your NGO's work. For instance, you can arrange a public meeting to explain your organization, outline its intentions, and answer any questions from the community.

If NGOs are not held publicly accountable for how they spend their money or for their actions, the public may believe that an NGO is using its resources for personal gain or for corrupt purposes. To counteract this misperception, an organization can develop a code of conduct. A code of conduct is a public document that contributes to the transparency of your NGO by establishing definite standards of ethical behaviour, corporate governance, and financial transparency. A code of conduct differs from your NGO's bylaws because bylaws cover logistical and procedural protocol whereas the code of conduct refers to standards of ethical behaviour.

Your NGO may face resistance from your intended beneficiaries if they are averse to accepting aid. Many beneficiaries may be reluctant to admit they need assistance or to accept any form of aid. Conversely, they may admit the need, but feel that their own efforts are sufficient to address them. This challenge may be overcome with patience and a demonstrated commitment to respecting and understanding your beneficiaries' concerns. Incorporating your beneficiaries' input into your projects can also temper this resistance.

In cooperation with beneficiaries, remember to do the following:

- Seek out their advice;
- Value their perspectives;
- Respect their skills and knowledge;
- Include them in all stages of the project cycle;

- Establish trust and credibility; and
- Treat them as equal partners.

Although an NGO's primary relationship is with the community or beneficiaries it serves, whether as an advocate or as a direct service provider, a given NGO will also want to cultivate contacts with the for-profit business sector, with other NGOs, and with government agencies or officials.

Relations with other NGOs

Benefits: In order to expand the capacity of your NGO, you need to develop partnerships with other like-minded NGOs. There are many benefits to this form of cooperation. Often, limited NGO resources can compel like-minded organizations to work together to achieve their goals. In general, partnerships function better if one organization is considerably larger than the other or if each has a different area of expertise that is equally relevant and necessary to the completion of the project. Cooperation is facilitated among NGOs when each NGO has a well-defined role in the partnership.

For example, if one organization is large and focuses on political advocacy while a second, smaller organization seeks to enhance political awareness among women in a specific region, the two organizations could potentially have a very productive partnership. An example of a partnership could include a program that seeks to mobilize support for new legislation both with the politicians who will vote on the law and with their constituencies.

Another benefit from NGO partnerships is that smaller organizations can gain a lot of experience from working with larger, well-established NGOs. This is an excellent way for smaller NGOs to gain recognition and access to a broad network of contacts.

Challenges: Despite the benefits of collaborating with other NGOs, these relationships can be difficult. Difficulties often arise when NGOs are forced to compete over resources, projects, and public recognition. Because donor funding is limited, NGOs with similar missions may compete for a given grant. NGOs may also experience competition for recognition or prominence in the community. This presents a significant barrier to successful cooperation. However, the benefits of collaboration among like-minded organizations are far greater than those of working alone. Other challenges to building and maintaining networks with NGOs include:

- Being patient during the time-consuming process of getting individuals to agree on goals, objectives, and strategies;
- Building trust among members of other NGOs, since competition for funding may undermine trust;
- Managing logistics and informing all members of meetings, actions taken, results, and upcoming activities;
- Allocating resources and agreeing on rules for effective cooperation; and
- Maintaining a collaborative spirit among all members.

Networking

Networking will prove to be one of the most helpful activities for expanding your organization. Temporary alliances concerning single issues can accomplish short-term or very specific objectives. However, long-term and broad alliances among diverse groups are necessary when advocating for substantial or long-term institutional change. To begin networking, encourage your staff to attend conferences or seminars where other like-minded organizations will be in attendance.

Always carry business cards and do not be timid about striking up conversations with strangers about issues you have in common, similar experiences, or people you both know. Emphasize that you are always seeking to expand the scope of your organization and propose some form of potential cooperation. Keep all received business cards in an organized file and follow up with any contacts via e-mail or phone call after your initial meeting.

Events featuring speakers or discussion panels provide an opportunity for you to use the question-and-answer session to promote your NGO. Ask a question, give your name, and identify your organization.

This exposure will create interest in your organization and inform participants about your work. Despite potential barriers, partnering with like-minded NGOs and establishing a solid network of contacts in your industry are essential for expanding the capacity of your organization. Remember the following when partnering with other NGOs:

- Build trust and transparency into the process;
- Clearly identify roles and expectations;
- Emphasize common values and mission;
- Focus on mutual benefits for both NGOs;
- Establish and maintain a network of industry contacts; and
- Treat each other as equal partners.

GOVERNMENT RELATIONS

Cooperation between an NGO and the government can benefit both the organization and its official beneficiaries. The nature of these benefits will depend on the political context and the readiness of the government to partner with NGOs. Furthermore, the willingness of both sides to work together will depend on their respective perceptions regarding the benefits of cooperation.

One benefit of NGO-government partnerships is that governments have excellent access to some groups (students in public schools, for example) but very limited access to marginalized segments of the population—the very segments of the population that NGOs work with. Thus, by forming partnerships, NGOs and government agencies compensate for each other's weaknesses. Moreover, increasingly complex socio-economic problems, like widespread unemployment and lack of health services, require the combined resources of both government and NGOs to achieve lasting and effective solutions.

Challenges

Of all potential partners, government agencies may be the most challenging if there is significant distrust between NGOs and the government. NGOs often view governments as corrupt and ineffective, while governments may view NGOs as advocating positions contrary to their interests. Another challenge is that many governments do not respect the role of NGOs in the political process and consequently do not foster a legal and economic environment conducive to the successful operation of NGOs.

NGO-government relations are complicated by the unequal balance of power between the two. The government can greatly influence how an NGO operates through regulations and registration requirements. Moreover, in order to function effectively, NGOs rely on governments to establish and enforce basic laws and to make publicly available information about issues of social concern. Governments can also regulate the access NGOs have to international funding. Lastly, NGOs rely on governments to guarantee a free press and access to the media.

Ideally, because government policy is relevant to their work, NGOs should be incorporated into governmental policy-planning. However, one potential drawback when NGOs work with the government is that this can result in "weakening their legitimacy as independent voices for grassroots groups and their members." Moreover, government officials may not know how to incorporate NGOs into their planning process. Therefore, when deciding whether to work with the government to achieve change, an NGO must weigh the practical benefits of collaboration against the harm it might do to the organization's reputation.

Solutions

Some ways to encourage cooperation between NGOs and government include:

a. Stressing the urgency of the problem, including possible political consequences, such as a representative potentially losing the next election because he/she does not address the problem of the community;

b. Emphasizing why the government cannot address the problem alone and why your organization is uniquely positioned to do so;

c. Networking with government officials and establishing strong relationships between individuals in your organization and those in government agencies;

d. Exhibiting respect for and understanding of governmental structures and systems;

e. Establishing clear expectations and work distribution; and

f. Developing a common mission statement or guiding document.

NEGOTIATION

Cooperation always entails negotiation. Therefore, strong negotiation skills are critical to the success of your partnerships, whether with beneficiaries, businesses, other NGOs, or the government. Negotiation is a process whereby two or more parties resolve an issue, whether it be a dispute, a debate about a particular course of action, or a bargain over resources.

The first step in any negotiation is to analyse the situation, clarifying your interests and those of the other party, and identifying possible resolutions. Next, your organization will strategize how to respond to the other party. In the final stage, the parties meet and discuss the problem, debate options, and agree on a solution. Negotiations can be very tense and complicated if the parties do not follow certain core principles.

Core Principles

Separate the people from the problem: A common mistake in negotiation happens when parties confuse the problems of individuals with problems inherent in the discussion. In order to avoid this confusion, you must be able to identify the most common people-centred problems:

- Problems of perception constitute the most common cause of conflicts. Make every effort to understand the perspective, viewpoint, and interpretation of your counterpart.
- Problems of emotion arise because many individuals identify personally with their interests or position and will react with anger or fear when they feel threatened. Acknowledge the emotions and try to understand their source.
- Problems of communication also commonly cause disputes. Employ active listening techniques to minimize communication problems. Give the speaker your full attention and periodically summarize his or her points to ensure you understand; you can understand your counterpart and still disagree with her.

Focus on interests rather than positions: Instead of traditional negotiation, where one side wins and the other loses, try to emphasize principles over positions. Seek out a "win-win" situation.

Define the problem in terms of the principles or interests of each side instead of in terms of their specific positions. Strict positions often make compromise or a "win-win" situation impossible.

Look for solutions that will reconcile the interests of both sides. For example, the above-mentioned case study in negotiation regarding the minority and majority group illustrates a win-win situation, where the solution satisfies the interests of both groups although not their initial positions.

Generate a variety of options before settling on an agreement: In order to ensure the best possible solution, both parties must consider as many options as possible. Both sides can cultivate an environment where creative proposals are welcome. Each side can also agree on a common definition of the problem, analyse the problem, consider general approaches to solving the problem, and then examine the potential consequences of specific actions. Negotiation seeks to build consensus among the participating parties. Effective consensus-building techniques can:

- Help structure discussion and keep it from going in circles;
- Downplay the link between an idea and its "author";
- Reduce the tendency to conform to group opinion;
- Protect against reprisals for open disagreement;
- Encourage respect for strong opinions; and
- Allow valid options to be compared.

PROJECT DEVELOPMENT: DESIGN AND MANAGEMENT

Each project follows a general cycle called the project cycle. The project cycle is divided into two broad categories. The first is project design which entails preparation and planning. The second is project management which includes the execution of the project.

Project Design

Before writing a grant to obtain funding, you must design your project. Project design involves the preparation and planning stages of the project cycle.

Preparation: The significance of the preparation stage should not be underestimated. Most projects fail due to insufficient or flawed preparation. Thus, it is necessary to invest a sufficient amount of time, energy, and resources in the process. The first step in developing a concept for a project is to gather necessary information; you will need to decide what information you need, who you will consult, and how you plan to gather this information. It is important to establish the role the community will play in the project design process, and specifically to include the beneficiaries in your preparations; your organization will want to consult the people it is hoping to help in order to obtain their perspective and input on their own needs and ideas for change. You may also look to local experts or community members with extensive experience in areas related to your program. There are several ways you can gather this information, including interviews, questionnaires, focus groups, and case studies. Choose one or a combination of these methods to best fit your needs.

Consulting: Project preparation involves consultations with the community about their needs. When gathering information, you will want to include both quantitative and qualitative forms of data collection.

After gathering this general information you are ready to begin the needs assessment.

Needs Assessment: The needs assessment ensures that your project is necessary, timely, and will benefit the community you are trying to serve. The needs assessment can be summarized in a series of questions relevant to your NGO's intended goals and activities. A working group formed of members from your organization and the community could discuss these questions to address the community's needs. The needs assessment will build on the general information you already collected and may entail additional specific research.

Involving the Community

Developing a relationship with community members in which they feel free to honestly express themselves with members of your organization is not only beneficial in assessing their needs, but also helps gain the trust of those you most want to help. By asking community members about their needs, you are allowing their voices to be heard and are empowering them by including their input in your decision-making process. Involving the community demonstrates that your project is not controlled by outsiders who are unfamiliar with the particular strengths and constraints of the community. By involving community members in an ongoing dialogue, you will gain information that will be helpful to successfully building your NGO as well as fostering lasting relationships that show your commitment to the members of the community.

Needs Analysis

After conducting a needs assessment, the next step is to analyse and prioritize those needs in order to design a project that first addresses the most pressing needs. This step is referred to as a needs analysis. Needs analysis includes an analysis of the social, political, and economic situation of the community and region you are working with. It also analyzes the beneficiaries' situation and the specific problem the project wants to address. You may want to emphasize to community members that you value their opinion, even if you do not eventually decide to take their recommended course of action.

Goals and Objectives

Once you identify and analyse the purpose of your project (the need you will address), you then develop goals and objectives for the project. The goals and objectives of the individual project should reflect the goals and strategies of the organization as a whole. Objectives should be specific, measurable, realistic, and achievable within a certain amount of time. In developing clear goals and objectives, it is important to develop certain indicators. These indicators are empirically observable and measurable terms that allow NGOs to measure and evaluate their progress and foster transparency in their organization. Indicators are "parameters of change or results indicating to what extent the project objectives have been achieved." Thus, after gathering information, assessing and analyzing the needs of your organization and community, and outlining your goals and objectives, you will move on to the second stage of the project cycle and plan your project.

Planning

The planning stage consists of designing the project. This entails a series of actions, including determining which strategy will be used, which activities will be organized, and what time and financial constraints will affect the project. You should plan your project before you write your grant proposal.

When planning your project, design programs that build on your strengths. A strategy represents the overall approach your organization will take and details how you will employ your organization's strengths. The strategy is then divided into tactics, or details of what must be done and how to do it. Tactics address which specific activities will be organized, where, what skills and materials are needed, and how much time each activity will take.

Writing a Grant Proposal

The final action of the project planning stage is writing a grant proposal. Most donors have specific guidelines for writing a grant proposal and you must tailor your proposal to meet each donor's qualifications. A grant proposal includes information gathered in your preparation and needs assessment, information about your organization, specific details of the project design, and an itemized budget. Once funding is secured, you execute and manage the project.

Project Management

Executing your project requires strong project management skills.

Execution: Execution is the stage where the project is carried out. Your preparation and planning will significantly impact the success of your project's execution. The particular execution of each project will vary widely. However, all project managers face challenges in this stage as many unexpected complications may arise. These challenges include, but are not limited to, the following:

- Managing your team successfully;
- Documenting the project;
- Maintaining flexibility in the face of new developments;
- Delegating responsibilities clearly and efficiently;
- Keeping everyone on time and meeting all deadlines;

- Maintaining good contact with partners;
- Making decisions;
- Coordinating and organizing all individuals and resources; and
- Monitoring and evaluating your success and impact.

Monitoring and Evaluation

Periodically, throughout the process of implementing the project, you will want a team from your organization to take the time to review the status of the project. Most donors require periodic reports from grant recipients and many have specific guidelines that must be closely followed.

The status review measures the results of the activities already implemented against the initial plan and identifies possible problems that need to be addressed. Upon the completion of the project, it is necessary to evaluate your organization's performance in the form of a narrative report. The format will vary by donor, but the general components of a narrative report are as follows:

- Introduction: basic information about the community need your project addressed and the general mission of your organization;
- Objectives and activities planned;
- Results: describes which objectives were met and what activities were successful;
- Problems, challenges, and changes or adaptations you had to make.
- Lessons learned;
- Feedback from beneficiaries about the project.
- Follow-up plans; and

- Annexes: copies of materials developed for the project.

The narrative report will show your donor your successes. It also allows your organization to document the progress made and the lessons learned. Reporting increases the development of your organization's capacity in future endeavours by offering potential donors or individuals interested in your NGO a chance to see your accomplishments and improvements.

NGO MANAGEMENT: STRATEGIC PLANNING

Strategic planning can be defined as "the process during which one determines where one wants to go, what one wants to do, how to get there, and when, including securing the necessary resources." Strategic planning starts with the organization's vision and mission statement. Based on its mission statement, long-term and short-term goals are set. The objective of strategic planning is to yield a realistic plan and program for achieving an NGO's goals. Moreover, strategic planning outlines an NGO's specific objectives, activities, and timeline as well as financial and staff requirements. Usually, the strategic plan is developed by a team of staff members from the NGO. Responsibilities of the strategic planning staff members include:

- Clarifying organizational mission and values;
- Identifying target population or beneficiaries as referred to in international humanitarian and NGO circles;
- Assessing the external context;
- Assessing the internal context;
- Identifying the strategic issues;

- Formulating strategies to manage these issues (creating options);
- Establishing an effective organizational vision for the future;
- Converting the vision into activity plans, budgets, and key result areas that can be monitored;
- Monitoring performance "actual characteristics" versus "expectations"; and
- Making adjustments to the plan.

The strategic planning process can be divided into four steps: (i) preparing to plan; (ii) environmental analysis; (iii) defining goals and strategies; and (iv) identifying needs and organizational capacity.

Preparing to Plan

Time spent in preparing the planning process will ensure the utility of the strategic plan and the future success of your organization. Preparation consists mainly of asking the right questions, such as:

- Who will be involved in the preparation process and how much influence will they have? When will that process take place?
- Who will be consulted to offer advice? Which external experts and which beneficiaries will be consulted? How much time will be devoted to the process?
- Who will handle the administrative duties?

You will also want to define the scope of your work according to the purpose of your NGO. You need to answer the following three questions to clarify your organization's capacity:

- What must the NGO do? What actions would coincide with the vision and mission statement?
- What can the NGO do? What is the capacity of the NGO, given its human and financial resources? For example, if your mission is to help legal awareness of human rights, you must determine what activities your organization will do to further your mission (e.g., issuing pamphlets, holding training seminars).
- What needs to be done? What do the community and beneficiaries need from the NGO?

After answering these questions, the next step in preparing a plan entails analyzing the external and internal context in which an NGO operates.

Contextual Analysis

The external context is the economic, political, and social situation in which your organization operates. You need to consider the benefits and constraints of working in your field, including legal restrictions and the social, cultural, and political backgrounds of your beneficiaries. In this step, you examine the problem you wish to address by analyzing its causes as well as by researching what other organizations or agencies are doing to help combat the problem. An analysis of the external context you work in provides a clear picture of the opportunities and constraints that will influence your strategic plan.

Analyzing the internal context of your organization is as important as examining the external context in which you work. In order to analyse the capabilities of your organization, it is best to determine what your organization's strengths and weaknesses are as well as what its past performance has been. This information will highlight the critical issues your organization faces and clarify the strategic plan you must adopt. You will also need to identify qualities that differentiate you from others in your field. Finally, examine the previous experience of your members or other NGOs' experiences, identifying lessons learned so as to best develop your organization's future plans.

Such external and internal analysis will improve your awareness of the important factors that affect your strategic planning.

Defining Goals and Objectives

Use your organization's vision and mission statements as a foundation for developing your strategic goals. Goals are defined as "enduring statements of direction that [strengthen] the mission statement and focus the organization's efforts." Building on your preparation and contextual analysis, you can define the goals and strategies you will pursue over the next few years. Addressing any internal capacity needs will be one of your goals. In order to do so, outline the human and financial resources that are currently available to you, the human and financial resources that you need, and examine the discrepancy between the two. Group discussions among your members and staff—where participants can offer their suggestions on how best to address any perceived problems—can yield strategies for how to fill any perceived gap. Your NGO should then develop a short-term internal capacity-building plan that outlines the gaps you have identified and the subsequent plans or programs that will be instituted to address them.

To develop additional goals, identify the specific issues and choices your organization and your beneficiaries will face over the next 2-3 years. You can do this by highlighting areas that need to be changed, particularly those weaknesses you previously identified in your contextual analysis.

The strategic goals you set should state what your organization wants to achieve during the specified time and how it intends to achieve those aims. The goals should be quantifiable, achievable, and in line with your vision and mission.

Developing a strategic goal is sometimes difficult because it reflects “a balance of two somewhat conflicting considerations— ambition and accountability.” A strategic goal should be “the most ambitious result (intended measurable change) that your NGO can make and for which it is willing to be held responsible.” These goals should then be prioritized in order of importance. This can be done by taking into consideration what the consequences would be if you did not address the problem.

Objectives are the means by which the goals are achieved. It is advisable to develop multiple objectives for each goal. Examples of objectives used to reach a particular goal include advocacy, project funding, public awareness campaigns, networking, and training seminars. A well-formulated objective should:

1. Mimic a format such as “to distribute a pamphlet,” or “to register 500 women to vote”;
2. Specify a single key result to be accomplished;
3. Specify a target completion date or time period; and
4. Make a real contribution towards achieving the relevant goal.

Identifying Financial Capacity

Lastly, you should examine the financial needs of your NGO. This process includes identifying the needs of your organization and your beneficiaries, and assessing the capacity of your organization to meet those needs. After identifying these needs, design a budget and estimate the costs of instituting your strategic plan. Outline the requirements of each program or strategy in terms of equipment, services, people, and materials by dividing each into essential and non-essential categories. Then, determine the cost of each requirement and calculate your organization's available funding. Finally, you should develop fundraising strategies to address any of your organization's financial needs.

6

NGO Leadership: The Governance-Management Partnership

ORGANISATIONAL LEADERSHIP

Organisational leadership is about organising collective action to meet organisational purpose.

In recent years increasing attention has been given to the exercise of leadership at every level in an organisation. The idea of such distributed leadership is particularly relevant in nongovernmental organisations, or nonprofit organisations, where people often work because they are attracted by the purpose, or mission, of the organisation.

The Leadership Center at MIT Sloan School of Management has developed a 'a pragmatic, research-based model of how successful leaders at every level actually work'. Their 4 Capabilities Leadership Framework (FCF) defines four critical components of leadership:

Sensemaking: making sense of the world around us,

coming to understand the context in which we are operating.

Relating: developing key relationships within and across organizations.

Visioning: creating a compelling picture of the future.

Inventing: designing new ways of working together to realize the vision.

In any organisation those holding formal leadership roles at governance and management level have particular responsibility and opportunity to fulfil these functions. In NGOs they are responsible for deciding and guiding the organisation's strategy at the following levels:

Organisational effectiveness comes from alignment of collective effort in relation to the organisation's vision, mission and values.

Vision

A defining characteristic of NGOs or nonprofits is that they are vision/mission/values-driven. Fulfilling a mission relating to a particular vision of the community/society/world – rather than profit – is their bottom line, and people are generally motivated to work for/in/with the organisation because they share its vision of the future.

'A vision helps unite people towards a purpose. Creating and living a vision is the role of leaders in organisations. They have to espouse it and help others to believe it. Visions are aesthetic and moral, they come from within as well as outside.' (Brefi Group, 2010)

Mission

"A clear, agreed-upon mission statement is one of the

four primary characteristics of successful non-profit organizations" Niven (2003, p102)

The organisation's mission is the reason for its existence. It is the organisation's contribution to realising the vision.

According to Peter Drucker (1990) a mission must:

- relate to an organization's strength: 'Do better what you already do well-if it's the right thing to do'
- relate to external opportunities, needs: 'Where can we, with the limited resources we have-and I don't just mean people and money, but also competence-really make a difference, really set a new standard?'
- be something we can believe in

Deciding on the organisation's mission involves questions such as:

'What are the opportunities, the needs?'

'Do they fit us?'

'Are we likely to do a decent job?'

'Are we competent?'

'Do they match our strengths?'

'Do we really believe in this?'

To fulfil its role in communicating purpose to critical stakeholders, a mission statement needs to be reasonably succinct and compelling.

For example, faced with a global written-by-committee Amnesty International 'mission statement'

To make the best contribution New Zealanders can to ending some of the worst violations of human rights worldwide.

Values

Connected intimately to the vision of the community/society/world to which they are trying to contribute are the values that guide the organisation in the fulfilment of its mission.

Steve Jobs, CEO of Apple Computer, Inc., once remarked, 'The only thing that works is management by values. Find people who are competent and really bright, but more importantly, people who care exactly about the same thing you care about.' (Koteinikov, 2008)

Values are the beliefs of an organisation, the expression of what it stands for and how it will conduct itself. Values are the core of an organisation's being. They underpin policies, objectives, procedures and strategies because they provide an anchor and a reference point for all things that happen. (Brefi Group, 2010)

A growing number of NGOs are recognising the usefulness of referencing *human rights* in their values statements. The community/society/world they envisage is generally one based on human dignity and freedom, and the cross-culturally negotiated, internationally agreed human rights framework contributes standards based on widely shared values that can readily be applied to the mission and life of the organisation.

Strategy

The broad coherent priorities you plan to pursue in order to achieve your mission – consistent with your unique situation and responding effectively to your challenges and opportunities. (Niven, 2003)

Development of strategy often involves difficult choices for NGOs inspired by a vision for the world.

"Some nonprofits develop a big pile of well-intentioned programs, ideas and directions that try to respond to every need and opportunity that comes along and might vaguely fit under their mission. There is always a reason to do something that no one else is willing to do if it relates to the mission. The harder thing, as is often pointed out in strategy discussions, is to have enough of a strategy to know when to say no, when to drop things, pass up opportunities. Understand that, yes, a need might be real, but you might not be the best response to it." (Bill Ryan, in Niven p128)

Paul Niven suggests the following steps to develop organisational strategy:

Review

View your organization from an historical perspective. Chronicle the history of your public or nonprofit agency from its earliest developments to the present-day realities you face. Along the way you can document programs and services you've offered, milestones reached, any shifting priorities, and external events such as demographic or legislative changes. (p134)

Consider using the Appreciative Inquiry approach to balance the deck. (p135)... []

Conduct stakeholder analysis

Who are the organisation's key stakeholders? What do they value in the organisation's work? How do they rate the organisation's performance? Which stakeholder expectations must be met?

Identify strategic issues

[F]undamental policy questions or critical challenges that affect an organization's mandates, mission, and values; product or service level and mix; clients, users, or payers; or cost, financing, organization, or management.

Strategic issues are those that

- appear on the agenda of your board or elected officials and leaders.
- are longer term in nature.
- affect the entire organization.
- have significant financial ramifications.
- may require new programs or services to address.
- are "hot buttons" for key stakeholders.
- may involve additional staff. (p138)

Develop strategies

Strategies may emerge from considering questions such as:

- What are the practical alternatives we could pursue to address this issue?
- What potential barriers exist in the realization of the alternatives?
- What action steps might we take to achieve the alternatives or overcome the barriers to their realization?
- What major actions must be taken within the next year (or two) to implement the action steps?
- What actions must be taken in the next six months, and who is responsible?

Developing organisational strategy requires time and involvement of the full NGO leadership – governors and managers. Retreat workshops – away from the hurly burly of day-to-day business – are often useful.

Although both boards and senior management must be involved in the development of strategy, the decisionmaking roles are distinct: it is the board's job to *decide* what the overall strategy is, and the management's job to *decide* how it is to be implemented.

THE NGO LEADERSHIP PARTNERSHIP

Effective NGOs are led by a powerful partnership of the board and chief executive. These notes describe that partnership, the contributions made by each party, and the shared leadership functions.

Before looking at this in more detail, it is useful to examine how the board-management partnership generally develops.

NGO leadership arrangements typically change over time as the NGO grows in scale.

As stakeholders require greater accountability in return for their investment of time and money, a more clearly differentiated governance role develops.

Adjustments in role and power balances can be difficult.

With increasing stakeholder expectations for NGO effectiveness, there has been a drive for greater professionalism in both leadership roles.

LEADERSHIP CONFUSION

A close reading of the section above on *Terminology and Key Concepts* readily points to a problem: there is clear overlap between definitions of 'leadership', 'governance' and 'management'.

In the late 1990s two UK organizations carried out one of the most extensive studies of governance. ACENVO (the UK Association of Chief Executives of National Voluntary Organisations) and the Charity Commission (the regulatory body for charitable NGOs in England) based their study on surveys completed by 100 Chairs and 260 CEOs, best/worst case studies involving 14 Chairs and 13 CEOs, discussion groups, and an independent review team.

In the resulting report, *Partners in Leadership*, the review team cited the following quotes from NGO leaders:

'I sometimes feel that the board members have all of the responsibility but the chief executive has all of the power' (Chair)

'If I am honest I can only exercise governance to the extent the chief executive allows me through the information he gives me' (Chair)

'A chair can quite easily get rid of an incompetent chief executive (procedures and good practice go out of the window!), but a director can't get rid of an incompetent chair.' (chief executive)

'As a chief executive I give positive feedback to the staff, but there's no one giving me positive feedback on my performance or the performance of the organisation' (chief executive)

'Board members don't always appreciate the role of the director. There is sometimes a perception that the director is one of us, but they also get paid. The fact that I'm paid is considered somehow "dirty".' (chief executive)

'The lines between policy and operations are always grey' (chief executive)

'It is the board which must sustain continuity of fundamental aims, values, visions and policies. Too often it is the chief executive who is custodian of the values and vision.' (chair)

A leading New Zealand writer on governance, Doug Matheson reports that 'dysfunctional relationships between board directors/chairman and chief executives are a major concern of chief executives today', with commonly cited problems such as:

1. Board members not familiar with the difference between governance and management, get too involved in what are essentially management decisions.
2. Board meetings feel like a game of 'spot the mistake' where board members get bogged down in historical detail at the cost of addressing larger issues and the future.
3. An adversarial director/chief executive relationship; board members nit-picky and distant from the reality of the business.
4. Board members 'who focus on what the organization can do for them rather than what they can do for the organization.'
5. Board members' 'increasing concern with compliance is making them more risk-averse and causing them to focus on history at the expense of the future.'
6. Many board members adopt an old 'command & control' approach to managing the CEO, creating problems in the relationship.

All too often the governance-management relationship

looks like this: The effectiveness of NGOs is often undermined by lack of clarity concerning the respective contributions of board and management to the leadership of the NGO.

The value-adding board

'Our board is like a bunch of ants running around having meetings on top of a log carried by a turbulent current swiftly down the river. The ants think they are steering the log.' (Senior Vice President of a Fortune 500 company in Leighton & Thain (1997)

"To be effective, a non-profit needs a strong board, but a board that does the board's work.

'A board that understands its real obligations and sets goals for its own performance won't meddle. But if you leave the board's role open and undefined, you'll get one that interferes with details and yet doesn't do its job.' (Peter Drucker)

As many organisations start with do-ers and managers before a formalised board is developed, defining the role of the board – as distinct from 'management' – is often problematic. What is the contribution of the board?

The 'man who invented management', Peter Drucker, said that 'to be effective, a non-profit needs a strong board, but a board that does the board's work. He argues that the role of the board is to

- help think through the institution's mission, be the guardian of that mission, and to make sure the organization lives up to its basic commitment;
- make sure the non-profit has competent management-and the right management;
- appraise the performance of the organization.

He adds that, in a crisis, the board members may have to be firefighters. (p123)

Doug Matheson (2004), who has written extensively about governance in the corporate, public and nonprofit sectors in New Zealand, points out that the board's contribution to the organisation's leadership is based on its detachment from day-to-day management of operations. He says the board should bring

- a helicopter view of the organisation
- an independent check on management on behalf of key stakeholders
- breadth of experience, contacts...

To govern, he says, the board must

- ensure the organisation justifies its existence and does no harm;
- define and maintain, through management, the organisation's values and culture, including a strong customer-focus;
- understand the organization, operating environment, and risks and threats facing it;
- have measurements, benchmarking and understanding of how the organisation compares with the best;
- be satisfied that the culture can deliver the outcomes expected (p23)

Governance, Matheson says, is about ensuring

- direction
- performance
- transparency

- accountability (p41)

One of the most helpful distinctions in the governance-management relationship focuses on ends and means.

John Carver makes the case for boards to focus on the development of 'governance policies' (as opposed to management policies) – ie policies relating to

- the end results the organisation seeks to achieve ('ends policies')
- the means that management must avoid ('limitations policies')
- the operations of the board itself.

The agreed values of the organisation are a key guide to the means that are acceptable/unacceptable.

This approach gives maximum scope for management to determine, on the basis of their expertise and day-to-day familiarity with the operations of the organisation, how strategy is to be implemented to achieve the ends agreed by the board.

After deciding on the desired ends and the unacceptable means, the key task for the board becomes communicating these policies and checking adherence.

Promoting the organisation and its mission amongst critical audiences, especially by drawing on influential contacts, is a key role for board members. In many NGOs this extends to helping generate income.

THE BOARD-CEO RELATIONSHIP

'The relationship between the board and the chief executive is the most important part of the governance role; it can either bring out the best results in everyone or can destroy the organization.' (Matheson p167) It is often said that the most important board decision is the appointment of the CEO – the person charged with meeting the ends agreed by the board. It delegates day-to-day operations to the CEO, who is accountable to the board for the organisation's performance. It is the only staff appointment made by the board, although board members may be involved in the selection process of other staff at the invitation of the CEO.

Clarity around the roles of the board, and the CEO it appoints, is critical. The relationship may be described in the following way:

It is important to note that the board is a collective decisionmaking body, and CEO accountability is to the board as a whole, not to specific members, including the chair.

The board has an obligation to its stakeholders to ensure that under the CEO the organisation is being effective in realising its mission. The board can and should be both a check on the performance of the CEO on behalf of the organisation's stakeholders. The NGO board should also be a valuable sounding board to be accessed by the CEO and senior management.

Best practice: the board-CEO partnership

The 1998 ACENVO study reported that the most effective NGOs were characterised by a stronger and more dynamic partnership than might be understood from this description of the respective leadership roles.

Amnesty International case study

As part of a process to overcome persistent perceptions that the *'real'* Amnesty International leadership was *either* in the hands of the Executive Committee elected by the volunteer membership *or* in the hands of an increasingly professionalised staff under the Executive Director, the New Zealand section developed a joint leadership model in the late 1990s based on the ACENVO recommendations and other NGO leadership literature.

Adoption of a shared leadership model was crucial in ending damaging tensions in Amnesty's international movement concerning the respective roles of the board (International Executive Committee) and CEO (Secretary General).

Many 'boundary disputes' between boards and CEOs can be managed when 'decisionmaking' is seen as distinct from 'input'.

Although *deciding* 'ends' such as the mission and organisational vision is a matter for the board, management's input can and should be substantial in an NGO.

Similarly, the advice of individual board members concerning operational matters can be invaluable, as long as all remember that decisionmaking on such matters remains with managers.

A TOOL FOR THE LEADERSHIP PARTNERSHIP

But how can strategy best be articulated, communicated and monitored by the leadership?

Robert Kaplan and David Norton have developed a management system for the 'strategy-focused organisation' that a growing number of NGOs in North America and Europe have found useful.

In the early 1990s Kaplan and Norton (Harvard Business School) were investigating the shortcomings of traditional financial measures as indicators of corporate performance. Traditional financial measures tend to lag behind critical developments, providing information that is out of date and sometimes too late to prompt needed changes. Non-financial measures, relating for example to investment in research and development, are often a critical indicator of the organisation's future. A *Balanced Scorecard* includes critical non-financial and lead indicators of performance at various levels of the organisation.

This approach makes sense in corporates (half the Fortune 1000 companies are estimated to use it); it makes even more sense for nonprofit organisations, where mission impact, rather than profit, is 'the bottom line'.

From work on 'balanced scorecards' Kaplan and Norton developed other invaluable tools – such as 'strategy maps' that communicate the key cause-and-effect linkages between measures from differing perspectives of the organisation.

The one-page strategy map is built by answering a range of critical questions:

Organisations have found that the resulting map is a key tool in communicating the organisation's strategy to internal and external stakeholders, helping to develop the necessary alignment of effort within the organisation to achieve the intended results.

On the basis that 'you get what you measure', measurable strategic objectives are developed for each level of the strategy map which make up the 'balanced scorecard' that is tracked.

The strategy map and balanced scorecard becomes the key strategy tool for both board and management, becoming the focus for annual and quarterly review and planning sessions.

The overall strategy – including top-level objectives, measures and targets – is decided at board level; 'cascaded' versions of the maps and scorecard, showing higher degrees of specificity and relevance to particular teams and individuals, become the tools used by management with staff.

NGOS, AND THE CHANGING PATTERN OF DIPLOMACY

A good deal of contestation has emerged about the nature of international leadership in the post-Cold War period. This debate is especially prevalent with respect to the multilateral architecture generally and the activities of the United Nations more specifically. As the global system underwent a major transformation in the late 1980s and early 1990s, a widely shared view developed of the United Nations moving to the forefront of an expanded form of global governance. As played out over the subsequent decade, though, progress towards this goal has become far-more convoluted. Instead of a sense of comprehensive achievement, generated by the passing of the East/West ideological/military divide, the process of transition has been far more complex, uneven, and awkward. The challenges in the way of creating and maintaining new forms of consensus-building, multi-centred governance networks and the negotiation of rules based on transparency and accountability remain formidable. Yet signs of transformation are visible in terms of the pattern of collective decision-making. The brake on the evolution of international organization remains the structural constraints imposed by the hierarchical state system, and the embedded role of agenda-setting among the established powers.' The motor for this dynamic of change, by way of contrast, has become the agency of innovative and non-liegemonic diplomacy. Given enhanced freedom from the disciplines of the Cold War era, room has opened up for a variety of actors in an array of areas. While far from unrestricted, the hallmark of this diplomacy has become its form (with a heavy emphasis on coalition-building), scope (its extension from the economic and the social into the security domain), and its intensity.

THE FRUSTRATIONS OF TOP-DOWN LEADERSHIP

This mixture of obstacles and momentum is provoked and underscored by a number of theoretical and policy-related questions concerning the source and application of leadership in the post-Cold War period. Most practitioners and academic/journalistic observers took it as a given that leadership would continue for the most part to emanate in a top-down fashion from the core permanent members of the UN Security Council, the so-called P5 states, as a "trusteeship of the powerful".' This type of arrangement would allow efficiency and order, if not necessarily equity and justice. As Robert Jervis suggested in 1993: "Concerts have provided a significant measure of security in the past and the conditions for establishing related arrangements are propitious."'

By moving its role to centre stage in the burst of enthusiasm for the creation of the "new world order", the performance of the United Nations seemed to match these expectations. As the Security Council became engaged in a widened cluster of focused problem-solving activities, a tilt took place in the overall image of the United Nations, from a "talking shop" to a constructive agent making a difference.' As the UN's agenda expanded, however, so did the gap between its capabilities and its commitments. These delivery problems were most pronounced in the peacekeeping/humanitarian intervention arena, as witnessed in Somalia, Rwanda, and the former Yugoslavia. Each of these operations suffered from weak and confused mandates and logistical deficiencies.

From a more comprehensive institutional perspective, this backlash became intertwined with a widening and deepening backlash against the hierarchical organizational structure of the United Nations itself. On a problem-solving basis the target of this criticism was the closed nature of the decision-making process; a process increasingly used not to drive initiatives forward but to block activity through backroom deals and the use of the "hidden veto".' On a more critical trajectory, the main focus has been on the question of whether or not the Security Council has become increasingly unrepresentative and illegitimate.

Indeed, it is this combination which constitutes the crucial ingredients of the chapters by Andy Knight and David Malone. Knight's contribution closely examines the critical conundrum of the Security Council. After a comprehensive review of the process of systemic change, featuring both the release of creativity in the immediate post-Cold War period and the subsequent sense of overstretch, Knight homes in on the issue of legitimacy and representation. As he argues: "For an apex body to be representative of the broader membership it must portray the values of the larger group; present the ideas or views of that group; be typical of that group's geographical make-up, population base, and political views; [and] act as a delegate of that group." The Security Council falls short on all of these criteria. Moreover, despite a proliferation of proposals to make the United Nations more transparent and equitable, there has been little in the way of tangible progress towards a reform agenda. Knight therefore ends with list of principles of his own which would not only be normatively attractive but provide a sound instrumental basis for a restructuring project for the Security Council.

Malone's starting point is the blockage imparted to the UN system by the informal process within the evolving design of the Security Council. Reinforcing the argument made by Knight, Malone points to the unanticipated consequences of the post-Cold War settlement in terms of the marginalization of many member states because of the privileging of private consultations between the UN Secretariat and the P5.

In contradiction to this image of exclusion, however, Malone also points to a number of countervailing trends central to the thematic structure of this book. Malone highlights in some detail the ability of NGOs to exploit new spaces in the international architecture to win access and input on selective areas of decision-making. Although careful to underscore the unevenness of this process, Malone captures the tensions between closure and immobilization and openness and innovation found within the UN system.

Part and parcel of this notion of duality is Malone's depiction of middle states or like-minded states within the UN system. Having lost a good part of their traditional role as go-betweens or helpful fixers, this cluster of countries is portrayed as having the will and capacity for issue-specific forms of leadership.

This prevailing sense of ambivalence about the terms of settlement in the post-Cold War system has been accentuated by growing confusion and concern about the style of US leadership. Through any lens of waning hegemony (or, to use Rugaie's term. "hegemonic defection"), scenarios opened up concerning the possibility of a collaborative arrangement forming at the top of the international system. From this perspective, the future held the prospect of some condominium with a strong element of joint responsibility and burden-sharing. Other lenses, nonetheless, provided very different images of American behaviour. One dominant alternative image has been that of "renewal" and/or "triumphalism" on the part of the USA.' A US-driven "new world order", or at the very least a US-centred "assertive multilateralism", contains some putative potential to be viewed as a benign force in the international arena. But this interpretation remains far from universally shared, with opinion in other countries varying "from agreement, to scepticism, to downright disbelief". Still another image is that of a heightened shift towards parochial introspection and insularity, with a marked withdrawal of the USA from its commitment to the United Nations and its own internationalist tradition. Signs of these latter two scenarios extend from the declaratory to the operational, as epitomized by the drawn-out saga concerning the USA's insistence on the right of taking military actions outside the United Nations, and its approach to UN dues.

Whatever scenario is favoured, the bottom line is that the US international personality and profile remain highly exceptional. As James Reed argues, the USA makes no pretence to be "like-minded" in either its coalition or issue-based behaviour. Unlike the cluster of middle countries that constitutes the bulk of the "like-minded" constellation, the USA not only possesses a global reach but massive hard power resources. Given its unique identity and multiple set of interests, consequently, the USA's opposition to the best-known initiatives associated with the "new diplomacy" (land-mines and the International Criminal Court) may come as no surprise. As Reed demonstrates in his chapter, though, the USA's estrangement from the United Nations and multilateral global governance goes much deeper than situational conditions. According to Reed, the key behind the USA's estrangement can be found in the structure of American society.

Having demonstrated the gap between the USA and the like-minded countries, Reed extends his argument to catch another important component of this puzzle. If "un-like-minded" as a state or country, the USA nonetheless contains a mass of "like-minded" citizens who have forged transnational linkages on an issue-by-issue basis. Ted Turner, Bill Gates, and other members of the American business elite remain highly international in their outlook. The Vietnam Veterans of America and Jody Williams have been at the core of the International Campaign to Ban Land-mines. US-centred groups such as Human Rights Watch and the Lawyers Committee for Human Rights moved to the forefront of the campaign for the ICC.

DIPLOMATIC INITIATIVES FROM BELOW

In rehearsing the manner by which international leadership is shapeshifting, this chapter looks at alternative sources of initiative and innovation. Animating this discussion is the argument that there is a need to look at how sources of leadership "from below" have adapted to change and modified their tactics to (re)work the UN system better. One longstanding source of alternative leadership, as suggested above, is located among the group of countries termed the traditional first followers of the UN system in the ranks of secondary states. This sense of commitment among this cluster of middle or like-minded states came out in diverse areas such as peacekeeping, and within the economic and social agendas. It also came out in the willingness of this cohort of states to put their money where their mouth is in terms of the payment of UN fees, contributions to specific UN operations, etc. While lacking the power capabilities of the inner circle of states at the apex of the global hierarchy, some compensatory element has been provided through diplomatic skill and focused use of resources. In the case of the United Nations, this active engagement by the like-minded revolved around a multiplicity of activities (as exemplified by the Canadian approach), such as "getting together sponsors for compromise resolutions, lobbying to avoid dangerous conflicts, collaboration with the efforts of the Secretary-General, and in a thousand ways seeking to reduce tension".

An awareness of the functional abilities displayed by this set of secondary countries should not minimize the constraints under which they had to operate. Self-selected like-minded countries such as Canada, Australia, and the Nordic countries were unrepresentative of the Wider society of nations. Not only were they developed countries, with membership in the Western European and Other group (WEO) within the United Nations, but they were countries which straddled regions. Such distinguishing characteristics disconnected these countries from other putative coalition partners among the less developed countries (such as India, Indonesia, Nigeria, and Mexico) through the 1970s and 1980s. Even in disagreement, these like-minded countries could in foreign policy terms be considered the USA's loyal opposition in the international system. Structurally, the space available for these countries to make a difference remained severely bounded by the context of the Cold War and the system of tight bipolarity. What influence these countries had in international affairs contained the distinctive flavour of both leadership and followership.

A key argument in this volume is that the character of this source of innovation and initiative is in the process of being transformed. With the release of many of the disciplines of the Cold War, like-mindedness has become more agile. The role of the gadfly long built into the like-minded concept has become far more accentuated, with the best known of these coalitions of the willing directed towards nudging and tweaking the P5 and especially the USA on selected issues in a determined and time sensitive manner. The range of candidates for like-minded status has also expanded. From a narrow and well-established cohort of countries, the scope for possible coalition partners has become far more inclusive. The element of continuity that has remained, and indeed has been reinforced, through this changing dynamic highlights the limitations of its issue, specific nature. Instead of providing leadership everywhere and on everything, an element of selection has come into play in a more explicit fashion. In other words, a form of country/activity differentiation is made by which individual countries make a choice as to which functional areas they will specialize in. This niche orientation offers secondary countries both an instrument and a rationalization for targeting their behaviour in a segmented fashion. As Gareth Evans, the former Australian Foreign Minister, has observed, niche diplomacy involves "concentrating resources in specific areas best able to generate returns worth having, rather than trying to cover the field".

This country-specific source of leadership has been supplemented, in turn, by the expanding diplomatic role of civil society generally and NGOs more specifically. One prominent former UK diplomat, in a book entitled *Positive Diplomacy*, has argued that: "Good governance depends increasingly on non-governmental factors." A similar message has been delivered by the UN Secretary-General Kofi Annan. Embracing non-governmental organizations as "essential partners of the United Nations", he defined their role in a multifaceted way, salient "not only in mobilizing public opinion, but also in the process of deliberation and policy formation and-even more important-in the execution of policies, in work on the ground".

CONCEPTUALIZING A NEW MODEL OF INTERACTIVE LEADERSHIP

Having laid out the potential for innovation, it becomes contingent to examine how these alternative sources of leadership have been expressed through the UN system. The working assumption here is that the relative (though far from absolute) shift from a concentrated top-down to a multifaceted bottom-up mode of leadership merits more detailed research. Indeed, this type of diplomatic practice has become so prevalent, fluid and fast-moving that it has raced ahead of intellectual formulations. A period of catching up is therefore required. At a conceptual level, the shift must be examined as a critical response to the status quo." Certainly, the shift represents an attempt to look beyond the status quo. Unlike more radical challenges to the international system, however, this alternative source of leadership has not been incorporated into a process of disengagement from the established rules and institutions. Although this expression of leadership exposes many limitations in that system, it does not constitute a bid to work from without. The focus remains very much one of trying to deal with frustrations and blockages in the UN system through new problem-solving techniques.

At an operational level, the style established by this alternative source of leadership comes to the fore in a number of ways. One dimension that needs to be examined is the intensity of this ascendant approach. There is a profound feeling of impatience at forms of diplomacy conducted at a slow speed-or no speed at all — behind closed doors. Rather than quiet diplomacy, the alternative leadership impulse is conducted via public diplomacy. Appeals are made directly and clearly over the heads of other negotiators/governments to opinion leaders and the mass public. Instead of the formality of traditional statecraft, considerable onus is placed on informal mechanisms via information technology. Ideas from the traditional leaders are no longer absorbed fully, if at all. Mission-oriented diplomacy, to use Gil Winham's words, is offered on an ad hoc basis, "when and where you, needed it".

Another dimension that requires attention is the form of this diplomatic approach. The core component that needs to be discussed here is the nature of the interaction between the secondary/like-minded countries and the NGO community. In some select cases, there does seem to be some evidence of the implementation of a concerted joint-venture strategy or strategic alliance. But in a variety of other cases, there is a considerable element of flexibility built into the approach, with a great deal of short-term assessment about the value-added benefits of striking a constructive arrangement on an issue-by-issue basis. In overall terms this pattern of interaction remains fuzzy, fragmentary, and awkward, but nevertheless vital and important. Like-minded countries and NGOs rub up against and off each other in an uneven fashion. Contacts and coalitions are built in an improvisational manner, but few in the way of coterminous roles are established. A premium is placed on bargaining and open-ended arrangements.

Another aspect of these alternative sources of leadership that needs discussion pertains to their multiple roles. One form of activity which stands out is that of a catalyst, by which the activity of NGOs stimulates corresponding or complementary activities by like-minded countries. At the core of this pattern is a triggering effect, in which the out-in-front behaviour on the part of like-minded countries and/or NGOs helps frame the agenda for action by the United Nations. This triggering component of the state-NGO relationship may be detected in a wide variety of cases and situations. For example, the reciprocal nature of this push-pull dynamic comes out strongly in the diplomatic efforts of NGOs with respect to other international conferences. As recognized by Baroness Chalker, the UK's former Conservative Minister for Overseas Development, much of the catalyst for action at the Beijing conference on women and development was stimulated by the NGOs' entrepreneurial ability to push this agenda forward:

at [Beijing], women's concerns moved up the policy-making agenda. Their relevance to a wide range of economic, political, and social problems was acknowledged. Much of the inspiration for change has come from thousands of women's groups all over the world. The impact of [Beijing] will depend largely on their success in working with men and with governments to turn words into action."

A second type of activity which stands out is that of an agent, a pattern by which NGOs take on some type of go-between or subcontracting facilitative role which supports the work of the United Nations. At a functional level, what appears novel is the amount of activity which may be described as micro-mediation. The prime illustration of this trend may be found in the area of negotiated access of relief deliveries in war zones either through non-protected and/or cross-border operations. As one insightful critic mentions, micro-mediation serves as the backbone of these types of operations: "to secure the consent of warring parties has become the principal means of establishing internationally mandated relief operations that cover all sides in an ongoing conflict".

A third form of activity which stands out is that of a joint manager, a pattern by which the activities of secondary countries and/or NGOs lend themselves to some type of enhanced institution-building. Integral to this dynamic is some further type of partnership or multi-party cooperative venture through which know-how is shared and some mode of formal or informal division of labour established. Arguably the best illustrations of this pattern of joint managership are located within the arena of Western responses to complex humanitarian emergencies. At the more formalized end of the institution-building scale, there exist firmly established partnerships in which government and NGOs work together. The exemplar of this integrative model is the Norwegian Emergency Preparedness System. (NOREPS).

A final dimension that merits discussion is the scope of this alternative source of leadership. What appears highly salient about the domain of these non-traditional sources is that they take account of the changing agenda of the international order. On the one hand, much of the focus of these alternative sources of leadership is on the ascendant issue areas in the economic and social domains. To be sure, one of the key elements of this volume will be to tease out case studies where this dynamic has already occurred.

One possible set of case studies comes out in the area of the interaction between trade, environmental, and labour "standards" issues, in which both secondary countries and NGOs have an increasingly high profile. Another potential cluster of case studies exists in the area of human rights. Children's rights come to mind as one good illustrative case study. The skill and determination of both secondary countries and NGOs in idea formulation and dissemination come out in their agenda-framing activities with respect to the development of a wide variety of protective regimes in this area.

On the other hand, a considerable amount of focus needs to be directed to the evolving debate about security. Driven by the sea change in circumstances created by the end of the Cold War, the "essentially contested" nature of the concept of security has surfaced in a provocative and comprehensive fashion. During the post-1945 era, there existed a consensual understanding about what the essence of security implied. In terms of both thinking and policy practice, the concept was applied to state security, and the security of states was predicated on the existence of some physical threat to territorial sovereignty. With the enormous changes in international politics precipitated by the collapse of the Soviet Union in 1991 and the end of the bipolar rivalry between the USA and the Soviet Union, this uniformity of opinion ended. With many of the secondary countries and NGOs in the lead of the rethinking, the concept of security has been extended to a much wider range of issues. Under this wider lens, security threats are more pervasive than traditional rivalries and confrontations between states. Removing the privileged status of the nation-state, alliance structures, and concerns of external aggression from other states, the definition of security is refined and expanded to cover the holisitic concerns of private citizens." The essence of security, or safety, from this standpoint rests on negative as well as positive criteria, namely the lack of insecurity on the part of individuals and groups.

PROTOTYPE OR ANOMALOUS CASE STUDIES?

Two case studies from the security domain provide suitable introductor entry points into the larger debate, in that these case studies highlight the breadth and diversity of the emergent alternative sources of leadership in the international architecture generally and the UN system more specifically. By providing a number of highly detailed contributions on these cases, we can better tease out the conceptual complexity and operational realities concerning the nature of the "new diplomacy" dynamic.

The first case study is the campaign for a global ban on anti-personnel land-mines. As laid out by Maxwell Cameron, the land-mines case was unique in a number of ways. Above all, it revealed how a combination of like-minded small and middle-sized states, as well as mine-affected states located mainly in the South, could work in partnership with transnational social movements and NGOs (in the International Campaign to Ban Land-mines) in particular. This combination of forces created a larger normative environment which non-signatories and the non-compliant could not ignore.

Looking at the case in further detail, it appears to fit the model laid out above. To begin with, the alternative sources of leadership acted as catalysts. The preparatory work of a constellation of NGOs was crucial in getting the campaign off the ground. Beginning in the early 1990s, the International Committee of the Red Cross (ICRC) was mobilized into action against the humanitarian "scourge" of land-mines by its field workers. Going beyond the organization's traditional low-key/technical mode of operation, the Red Cross took the lead in gathering a broad-based NGO coalition calling for a "total ban on the production, export, and use of anti-personnel mines". Eventually united under the auspices of the International Campaign to Ban Land-mines, this NGO coalition included the Vietnam Veterans of America, the German group Medico International, and the French group of Handicap International, together with Human Rights Watch and Physicians for Human Rights.

In terms of intensity, the campaign featured a good deal of speed and energy. Rather than waiting for results to happen via a lowest-common denominator diplomatic solution by governments, the NGOs constantly forced the pace of the negotiations through savvy use of publicity and the demand for real deadlines. When negotiations stalled through the ongoing arms control talks, the NGOs pressed for action through alternative channels. As Cameron points out, the pace of this process was unprecedented. No other multilateral disarmament treaty has ever come into being more rapidly.

Throughout this campaign a sense of strategic or at least tactical alliance stands out. Jody Williams lauded the actions of Canada and other like-minded countries for challenging the status quo. The main conclusion showcased by Cameron is that non-hegemonic states and transnational social movements can achieve diplomatic ends by working in partnership. The process in effect established the "basis for new mechanisms of horizontal accountability by bringing together like-minded states, in partnership with NGOs, outside of traditional arms control fora".

William Maley and Iver Neumann do much both to embellish and to nuance Cameron's conclusion. At the country-specific level, Maley's chapter deals with the Australian experience with the Ottawa process. As in a number of other countries, the issue of land-mines engaged the attention of diverse elements of Australian civil society and resulted in a broad campaign for total abolition. Mobilized under the umbrella organization, Australian Network of the International Campaign to Ban Land-mines, this network maintained a well-informed campaign, the expertise of which eventually trumped the claims of their bureaucratic opponents. Brought to the fore in particular through the hearings and work of the Joint Standing Committee on Treaties, Maley points out that there can be few better illustrations of deliberative democracy at work. At a more generalized level of analysis, Maley draws a number of wider conclusions from the land-mines process and its success in Australia.

Neumann is particularly interested in the relationship between the Norwegian Foreign Ministry and NGOs in the context of the land-mines initiative. As in many other countries, the Norwegian Foreign Ministry was caught between a NGO-1ed campaign and resistance in the military and defence establishment. On the one hand, sensitivity to the issue in the NGO community was triggered by the loss of some members of the Norwegian Afghan Committee (NAC) in a land-mines accident. On the other hand, the land-mines issue remained an idea that clashed with traditional Norwegian security policy, rooted in the experience of sharing a common border with Russia.

Yet Neumann points out as well that an analysis emphasizing a transnational NGO network pressuring a state to act is overly simplistic. States themselves have their own motivations for providing agency in terms of initiative and leadership. Not all states, of course, are able to adopt new diplomacy. One requirement is a richness of knowledge and skills. A second requirement is a good working relationship among different segments/ components of society and the state (for example, a good working relationship between intellectuals and NGOs and the Ministry of Defence, (Foreign Affairs). Third, financial capacity must exist. A final prerequisite for new diplomacy is the existence of good lines of contact between Northern states and the South.

A second case study of interest is the push for a permanent international criminal court. Again, the catalytic function of middle powers and NGOs stands out. From 1995 to 1998, a like-minded group of approximately 60 countries pushed for progress on this agenda. A core group-of countries supplemented this declaratory support by skilful legal work in developing a draft treaty. At the heart of this core group remained the self-identified cohort of traditional middle powers such as the Nordics, Australia, New Zealand, and Canada. Nonetheless, there was an additional group of non-traditional states within the leadership group. Of these states South Africa stands out. South Africa played a key role in the so-called group of "Lifeline Nations" advocating an independent court and independent prosecutor as opposed to an ICC under the control of the Security Council. Individual South Africans (notably Chief Justice Richard Goldstone) also played key roles. In all of this activity, furthermore, the like-minded states were supported by a wide variety of NGOs, ranging from the World Federalists to Amnesty International, Human Rights Watch, and the Lawyers Committee for Human Rights. The focal point of all this entrepreneurial and technical work was the June-July 1998 UN-sponsored Rome conference.

Alistair Edgar's chapter highlights in a number of ways the salience of the ICC for new diplomacy. Not only can the ICC campaign be identifie' with the growing visibility of partnerships between like-minded countries and NGOs, but the substance of the initiative itself is indicative of the process of transformation in the development of the international normative system. One of the hallmarks of the ICC is the independence of the prosecutor from the UN Security Council. Another is the potential for the erosion of state sovereignty through the court's jurisdiction. Still another is the implications of the UN Assembly vote allowing the court to have a role in individual countries.

If recognizing the new, Edgar cautions against any claim that the ICC is revolutionary. Indeed, he argues that in many ways the ICC is a blend of the new and the old. Edgar highlights the various ways by which the ICC comes up against the traditional world of power. While the court has jurisdiction, it is not clear whether or not the ICC can actually enforce its decisions.

Philip Nel argues that the establishment of the ICC brings another major dilemma into focus. Are the tendencies associated with the creation of the ICC part of a counter-hegemonic or a post-hegemonic movement? While a counter-hegemonic movement may lead to the creation of another form of dominance, a post-hegemonic movement may actually transform the character of the international system. From Nel's point of view, the establishment of the ICC should be seen as part of the latter process. While he acknowledges that the ICC is still contested by many developing countries, which feel that unchecked development of humanitarian intervention will contribute to arbitrary intervention, Nel concludes that the opportunities of the ICC as part of a new diplomacy outweigh these concerns. In terms of process, the ICC helps undermine the elitism associated with the P5 and the veto. At the ICC NGOs can claim representation. In normative terms, the ICC represents an excellent innovation to humanitarian law.

Narratives of these case studies are interesting in themselves. The more ambitious purpose of the research programme described in this volume, however, is to use these case studies to bring out some answers to bigger questions concerning global governance and the UN system. Arguably the most fundamental of these questions is whether these cases are prototypes of further activity of this sort, or anomalous episodes.

Certainly the pattern of activity found in the new

diplomacy *vis-a-vis* land-mines and the ICC does not exhaust the range of possible ways in which this dynamic is played out. To be fully comprehensive, the typology would have to be extended still further in terms of both actors and the range of issues to be covered. In form, one important dimension of new diplomacy that should not be neglected is so-called "triangular" diplomacy, including not only states and NGOs but states, NGOs, and the business community. In scope, this type of interaction moves beyond the security domain to encompass various aspects of commercial diplomacy.

Virginia Haufler's chapter provides comprehensive coverage of the impact on global governance of corporate codes of conduct and "co-regulation" between governments, the corporate community, and NGOs, Haufler shows the impressive scope of this process through a survey of both national and international regulatory and self-regularity practices. She argues that the adoption of corporate codes of conduct is uneven and depends on the differing effects of globalization. Among the incentives for companies to adopt codes of conduct are attitudes of shareholders, the danger of state-imposed codes, and reputation. In pushing for new forms of governance in the global workplace, NGOs have become a vital component in this dynamic. Nonetheless, as NGOs become embedded in their operations, Haufler suggests that these organizations face similar tests with respect to reputation and credibility.

Haufler argues that several core challenges remain in the process of trying to develop codes of conduct. What is included and what is left out? Who participates in the code's development? What is the best way to monitor such codes? In conclusion she notes that while business accepts some measure of government involvement, there exists fundamental distrust between business and NGOs, leaving little room for facilitation.

John English's chapter on the Canadian experience of trying to negotiate a code of conduct for Canadian companies elaborates on the question of opportunities and challenges. In common with other countries, the Canadian government has faced growing pressure by NGOs for a code of conduct in the apparel and related sectors. Yet despite its success in triggering the creation of a Task Force on Sweatshops, the mainstay organization in this campaign (the Ethical Trading Action Group or ETAG) has remained frustrated by the outcome of this process. The result was not a code but only loose guidelines companies could adopt for their use at the recommendation of the Retail Council (the representative organization of the business side). It lacked reference to ILO standards, did not address monitoring, and the freedom of association component was weak.

Instead of blaming the breakdown of this sort of initiative on the government's unresponsiveness to bottom-up approaches, the NGO assessment of what went wrong with the process is markedly state-centric, The ETAG complained that the Canadian government did not come through with needed funding, and was not willing to pressure business associations and companies in support of ILO core labour rights. The ETAG also pointed out to the obstacles posed by the international environment, because of both the limits imposed by Chinese sovereignty and the shadow of American legislation.

The chapter by Brian Hocking and Dominic Kelly is informed directly by the central theme running through this collection: the sources and impact of diplomatic innovation from multiple actors. More specifically, their chapter locates the changing role of the business community in the diplomatic milieu through a focused study on the activities of the International Chamber of Commerce via its relationship with the United Nations. In common with a number of the other contributors, Hocking and Kelly make some caveats to the extent of the actual "newness" in new diplomacy. Still, they emphasize that under conditions of globalization, the International Chamber of Commerce has become part of a multidimensional or polylateral diplomacy. Driving this new diplomacy on the part of the International Chamber of Commerce is not only a greater appreciation of the mutual benefits to be derived from this interactive process, but also the fact that multilateral strategies and norms are taken more seriously in the international system.

By their linkage of this component of new diplomacy to Kofi Annan's Global Compact initiative, Hocking and Kelly cut in as well to the additional question about the role of the UN Secretary-General. Whereas this volume has concentrated on the frustrations with the United Nations as a trigger for new forms of activity from outside the P5, there may be some other cases where the actions of key agents within the UN system may prove to be catalysts for accelerated action. Hocking and Kelly locate both the motivations and the institutional impetus for this type of advance in the case of the International Chamber of Commerce and the United Nations.

The final set of contributions to the volume returns to the question of where new diplomacy can become ripe in the security domain. One sign of an operational advance in this direction has been he Human Security Network initiated by Canada and Norway. Broader in scope than the Canada-Norway bilateral Lysoen Declaration, this initiative included 11 countries and nine NGOs at its first meeting in May 1999 at Bergen. On top of this broadly based initiative, as Deidre van der Merwe, Mark Malan, and Kim Richard Nossal testify, some considerable potential for cross-cutting partnerships on an issue-specific basis is available.

The van der Merwe and Malan chapter outlines existing initiatives aimed at the protection of children in armed conflict, and argues that they be complemented by a voluntary code of conduct. They concentrate their attention on three areas where codes of conduct could have a positive impact on the plight of children in armed conflict: in specific forms of humanitarian action, in small arms, and in the incorporation of and emphasis on the rights of children in armed conflict in military codes of conduct.

While van der Merwe and Malan acknowledge there exists abundant controversy about the feasibility and effectiveness of voluntary codes, they argue that these mechanisms increase ethical sensitivity and judgement. Codes are reflections of the morally permissive standards of conduct which members of a group make binding upon themselves. The principle that children's interests should be held in higher regard than military interests is viewed as being particularly valuable.

Nossal's chapter targets more specifically the role of innovative leadership in the case of UN sanctions and "conflict diamonds" in Angola. Nossal is fully aware of the defects of sanctions when used in an indiscriminate and blunt fashion. What his chapter demonstrates, however, is the salience of these instruments when mobilized in a smarter, sharper, and stronger fashion on an issue-specific basis. Replicating the triangular shape detected on codes of conduct, Nossal traces the links in an emergent partnership between NGOs (most notably Global Witness), a variety of like-minded states (including Britain), and, after some considerable initial reluctance, the global diamond industry generally and De Beers more specifically.

As a case study of new diplomacy in action, the issue of conflict diamonds underscores the relevance of the model depicted above. Catalysts, in terms of individual change agents, were on tap. Ail accentuated intensity was provided by the tactic of "naming and shaming". And some sophisticated division of labour was developed, as witnessed most clearly by the creation of the World Diamond Council in September 2000.

7

Overview of NGO Strategic Risk Management

These are hard, challenging times for NGOs around the world. Whether service or social change oriented, NGOs operate in dynamic economic, political, technological, and institutional environments. For NGOs devoted to development in both the North and South, with increasing frequency, their legitimacy is questioned and accountability demanded. Stakeholders and the broader society and governments are frequently asking NGO leaders about their impact on society? Ricardo Wilson-Grau is a management consultant and since 1993, a senior advisor with Novib, where he is responsible for researching and developing applications of strategic risk management.

These changes require that NGOs modify how they respond to the world and seek to shape it. Consequently, many development NGOs are altering their strategies, as the shift to rights-and results-based approaches exemplifies. Moreover, they are varying their strategies more frequently than in the past. Change, of course, has always been important in every organization's life. Indeed, for NGOs, change is absolutely essential; every NGO's mission statement commits it to improving some unacceptable aspect of the world. Change, however, brings with it uncertainty and risk.

Risk—The Simple and The Complex

The root word of risk, *risicare*, means "to dare." Daring to act audaciously is inherent to the lives of NGOs. Without taking risks, there is no innovation or social change. The nature of NGO work is to dare constantly to make decisions and act to achieve positive results, while daring to hazard bad outcomes. One of the beauties of the risk concept is its simplicity. As with anything occurring in the future, there is uncertainty about the results, desirable or undesirable; there are *consequences* of each good or bad result; and one needs to focus on the *probability* of positive and negative results. Of course, life cannot be so simple. There is an equally important and much more complex dimension to risk. Individuals, organizations, and societies are all unique. Thus, risk is rooted in specific historical contexts—from the political and psychological to the economic and environmental—that shape people's perceptions of the consequences and the probability of an uncertain event.

Business and local and national governments

Even in situations where there is a precise mathematical calculation of probabilities, people will act on their *beliefs* about the chances of good and bad results. Similarly, people take action based on their *preferences* for one result over another, even when they know precisely the potential benefits. Of course, when a judgment is about the uncertain future results of social change, the decision is especially subjective and risky.

Risk management is relatively new for NGOs. One reason is the ease NGO decision-makers have in confronting operational hazards that only one hundred years ago would have been terrifying. Insurance controls the damage caused by illness or accidents. Personnel access loans in case of personal or family emergencies.

The dangers of disaster that come with all new technology are more readily mitigated than ever before, as when NGOs use virus shields and back-up systems to protect computers against electronic attack or human error.. A second reason is that applying risk management to achieving upside results, and not solely avoiding the downside ones, is a recent innovation. In today's highly competitive and unpredictable environment, NGOs not only face major opportunities and new dangers to achieve their missions, but these positive and negative risks are arising much more rapidly than in the past and are becoming more complex. They must be managed as never before. Consequently, NGO decision-makers that use strategic risk management may actively nurture success and counter threats of failure.

Strategic Risk Management

In the last ten years, the concept of risk management has expanded from its origins in the insurance industry. It has extended into the fields of investment finance, medicine, environmental management, space science, and meteorology. Today, business and local and national governments apply risk management principles. The theory and practice has also grown from its original focus on exposure to negative risks to address positive risks as well. Building on traditional risk science, strategic risk management centres on a reinforcing, iterative process, a recycling sequence of steps for making and implementing decisions involving potential bad or good results.

- Clarifying what the organization seeks to achieve— *goals*.
- Identifying the principal opportunities and dangers that may affect achieving these goals— *uncertainties*.
- Assessing the likelihood that each opportunity or threat will materialize— *probabilities*.
- Calculating the extent of the resulting gain or loss to the organization from each opportunity or danger—magnitudes of the good or bad *consequences*.
- Weighing what the organization can do: 1) to increase the probability and the magnitude of the good consequences of each opportunity, and 2) to decrease the probability and the magnitude of the bad consequences of each danger—*risk management techniques* for each opportunity or threat.
- Deciding whether and how the organization is able to take these actions— *costs and benefits* of each technique.

This definition of risk is powerful. Instead of struggling to avoid all uncertainties— for that would be to avoid all chances of positive outcomes—an organization strives to increase the chances and size of positive outcomes while reducing the odds and magnitude of the negative outcomes. *This dual strategy is the essence of strategic risk management*. It contrasts with the narrow, negative traditional focus—merely preserving the organizations past achievements from future losses. While guarding against loss, the NGO that manages risk strategically takes carefully chosen chances, purposely mindful of the positive side of a potentially surprising future. An organization managing risk strategically dares to succeed.

A Tool for NGO Decision-makers

In recent years around the globe, NGO organizations that are committed to social change have strengthened their professional management to achieve their missions and long-term goals. NGO leaders once could safely assume that internal and external conditions with a potential major impact on their stakeholders, programs, property, income, and reputation would be stable for a year or two. No more. Currently and even more so in the future, the strategy is short term. For example, one major innovation in NGO management has been to introduce systems of strategic planning. Commonly, NGOs engage every three, four, or five years in this fundamental decisionmaking for achieving institutional goals. Increasingly, however, change is so rapid that managers at all levels of the organization must make decisions vital to achieving their missions outside the multi-year cycle. Now, monthly and even weekly, an NGO's entire management must adapt to and participate in incisive strategic thinking and prompt strategic action. In fact, virtually everyone in an NGO must continually understand, accept, and participate in actions sharply focused on achieving their organization's fundamental purpose and goals.

This is easier said than done. Organization-wide involvement with uncertainty can create feelings of apprehension and insecurity. Strategic risk management offers a tool to build understanding and enthusiasm for change. From the broader perspective of risk as *risicare,* an NGO's staff comes to understand that changes— some bad, some good—are not only inevitable, but the organization can thrive with these changes. Everyone comes to recognize that change, properly anticipated and wisely managed, while still posing possible dangers, is a potentially positive force. Uncertainty becomes something with an upside and a downside, something that can be managed not just by decreasing the potential for losses, but also by increasing the potential for gains.

Empowered by this broadened approach to uncertainty and change, an NGO's personnel quickly think beyond the merely negative, accident-centred, insuranceoriented concept of risk. Recognizing that changes can be positive, even surprisingly good and certainly necessary, an organization's staff can come to work with risk as an opportunity to achieve positive outcomes, daring to succeed as well as to fail.

Capacity-building Through Strategic Risk Management

Strategic risk management can enhance but never replace a development decisionmaker's knowledge, field experience, cross-cultural skills, and other personal abilities. More specifically, strategic risk management enables NGOs to enhance their capacities in three areas.

Information. In management, the information function is vital. In today's "knowledge societies," decision-makers are flooded with data and ideas. The technological possibilities are a temptation to nurture a false sense of security by attempting to process all available information. Of course, managers must constantly observe, consult, read, and listen. Strategic risk management, however, offers NGO decisionmakers a methodology for rapidly sifting through and selecting the most relevant information.

Action. Today, NGO managers must combine hard, in-depth analysis with fast decisions. Risk management enables a decision-maker to act even as she or he thinks. Past successes and failures are analysed not so much to know what happened or to explain why things are as they are, but primarily to take the best decision about new activities. Exercising risk principles enables a decision-maker to identify what to change and innovate in order to maximize gains and minimize losses today, tomorrow, and in the future. For strategic decisions, certainly the search for truth must be rigorous. Strategic risk management incorporates the rational perspective of science, but the purpose is to understand in order to decide, to set objectives and make plans, but not at the expense of acting on them.

Delegation. Never before has the need for subsidiarity been greater for development NGOs. Strategic risk management facilitates delegation because risk principles are applicable at all organizational levels. Strategic risk management enables decisionmakers to spread authority and responsibility upwards, downwards, and across. Everyone can be engaged in taking risks responsibly to achieve their work units' "missions" or long-term goals. Thus, for instance, in an organization where everyone uses a risk approach, senior program managers with substantial field experience will be able to delegate with greater confidence to junior staff. In addition, a quicklearning, self-critical program staff will develop faster.

Strategic risk management can enhance but never

replace a development decision-maker's knowledge, field experience, cross-cultural skills, and other personal abilities

In sum, traditional and strategic risk management both emphasize a proactive attitude towards risk-taking and employ similar methods of analysis and techniques for coping with risk. All risk-taking is based on logical analysis of essential information. Risk decisions also involve strongly reasoned beliefs and preferences about the probability and the importance of the desirable and undesirable outcomes. Thus, the advantages of both traditional and strategic approaches to risk combine art and science, integrating reasoning with intuition. The fundamental difference is that traditional risk management focuses on *only* threats of loss; strategic risk management encompasses *both* opportunities for gain and threats of loss. At best, traditional risk management can only keep an organization where it now is; strategic risk management enables an organization to advance and develop its potential.

STRATEGIC RISK MANAGEMENT AND GRANT-MAKING AT NOVIB

Founded in 1956, the Netherlands Organization for International Development Cooperation (Novib/Oxfam Netherlands) is a non-governmental foundation funded by the Dutch government and public. Novib's purpose is to encourage a world community in which socio-economic contradictions between rich and poor are eradicated, the wealth of the world is more justly divided, and people and population groups can learn about and come to respect each other's cultures, and in the interest of their own development, cooperate on the basis of shared responsibility and mutual solidarity. Furthermore, Novib is a member of Oxfam International, a confederation of 12 organizations working together with over 3,000 counterpart organizations in more than 100 countries to find lasting solutions to poverty, suffering and injustice. As do all the Oxfams, Novib takes a rights-based approach to achieve structural, enduring improvement in the quality of life of people. Every NGO must customize its use of strategic risk management in accordance with its mission and long-term goals, which pose special challenges for an organization that approaches grant-making from highly political and normative perspectives.

Grant-making Guided by Organizational Values Rather than by Partisan Ideology Novib works for changes in policies and their corresponding practices to modify the structures and relations of power that are obstacles to people exercising their political, civil, economic, social, and cultural rights. In every society and community, access and control of resources are structured in ways that benefit some individuals and groups and discriminate against others. Thus, the key to success of a rights based-approach to development and social justice is empowerment. Citizens and social organizations obtain the capacity to be significant actors in a process to change the structure and relations of power to benefit the many and not just a few dominant sectors. To contribute to these ends, Novib applies three institutional strategies.

Every NGO must customize

First and foremost, Novib is a donor to approximately 850 local organizations in more than 50 countries in Africa, Asia, Latin America, the former Soviet Union, and Eastern Europe. These grantees are NGOs who work directly with and for the poor and disenfranchised. The aim of this cooperation is to increase the capacity of people to exercise their individual and collective rights and to make decisions about control and use of material, human, intellectual, and financial resources. The support, however, is purely financial. Novib believes that because of the power of money, a donor-recipient partnership may be undermined if the grant-maker also attempts to provide these organizations with professional or technical assistance on ways and means to improve their performance. It can easily lead to dependence, disempowerment of the grantee, and strategic or organizational problems. Second, Novib strives to inform Dutch public opinion. It educates the Dutch public about the non-Western world by challenging conventional images and encouraging deeper insights concerning development. Novib also tries to make the cultures of the South accessible to the Dutch public through, for example, publishing books written by southern writers. Novib promotes the personal involvement of Dutch individuals and organizations in actions such as fair trade aimed at a more equitable distribution of the world's resources. Third, with the other Oxfams, Novib defends the interests of developing countries in the political and economic power centres of the West and tries to influence policy decisions in favour of the world's poor.

Novib bases its core work of grant-making on a strongly normative approach to development as cooperation between independent social actors. Institutional autonomy, mutual accountability, consultative decision making, and transparency between donor and grantee are the four pillars of Novib's relationships of development cooperation. Novib channels well over 80 percent of its annual budget of US$170 million to fund like-minded counterpart organizations. Novib does not make grants to individuals. The average annual value of a grant is around US$150,000, and Novib is highly flexible in its funding. Grantees largely decide where Novib's donation can do them the most good. In addition, Novib strives to fund its grantees in three-year cycles and frequently, for nine or more years. In the rapidly shifting environment of international development cooperation, however, throughout each year staff increasingly face strategic choices about what grantees to fund.

Changing Political Environment

As is the case with NGOs around the world, Novib's stakeholders increasingly expect to know what has been achieved with their support and involvement. Furthermore, Novib now competes for funding from its principal donor, the Dutch Ministry of Development Cooperation, based on the quality of results and not solely on professional grant-making. Consequently, since 2000, Novib has given much more emphasis than before to the results it strives to achieve. To this end, Novib is applying strategic risk management in a variety of areas of operational decisions. The principal area is grant appraisal. Novib realized that if grantees and Novib itself only practice traditional risk management, then Novib's grants might be relatively safe, but the potential for more significant impact in a rapidly changing environment would be limited.

In 1980s and 1990s, the quality of the partner organization was the guarantee of positive results. Novib approached this challenge with a checklist of what it considered good grantee practice. That instrument was designed to provide a reading of the health of an organization and the quality of the project it proposed that Novib fund. Novib's rationale was that the closer a grantee was to standards of organizational excellence, the more likely the grant would be used wisely and the project successfully implemented. Solidarity, the right strategy, and excellent management continue to be important but are no longer sufficient.

Novib and its grantees must demonstrate impact. Committed to this demanding task in often volatile circumstances, Novib realized that if grantees and Novib itself only practice traditional risk management, then Novib's grants might be relatively safe, but the potential for more significant impact in a rapidly changing environment would be limited.

To increase the magnitude of the results, Novib understood that it must dare to manage risks strategically and not bureaucratically if it were to contribute to development. Novib decided that the emerging concept of strategic risk management would offer an especially appropriate tool for managing its grant-making. This methodology permits holistic, non-linear and dynamic analysis and decision-making about the potential for results. Consequently, from 2001 to 2003, Novib researched and developed a grant appraisal methodology grounded in risk management science. From August 2003 through February 2004, Novib field-trained over one hundred of its grant makers and managers in the new methodology.

THE APPRAISAL PRODUCT—JUDGMENTS

In Novib, a team of two to three program officers, a financial officer, and a team secretary are responsible for the Novib portfolio in a country or region. They use an appraisal manual, the "Toolbox," to support them in formulating their risk judgments. The product—their strategic risk appraisal—is a narrative document of four to eight pages with three components.

The upside risks: the opportunity for cooperation

The starting point is the congruence between the positive *results* a grantee wishes to achieve and one or more strategic objectives of Novib for the country or region. The Novib team identify and interpret what the grantee wishes to achieve that will improve the quality of life of sectors affected by economic, social, and political inequality. In particular, the team explains what it believes is the potential contribution to changes in policies and practices. They also identify other positive *consequences* or "added social value" of the grantee's activities.

The positive consequences are the most important but not the only element of the opportunity for cooperation and for Novib to provide funding. The amount and duration of the grant also depends on the *probability* of success. Thus, the team looks hard at the counterpart organization's resources and track record and at the environment in which it operates. It identifies the capacity that the grantee has demonstrated to achieve similar results and to manage change. Furthermore, the team takes into account favourable external social actors and factors. With this foundation, the team formulates its judgment about the probability of this organization achieving its results.

The downside risks: the principal dangers to success

The second component of the appraisal is the downside risks or threats that endanger the success of the opportunity. Novib calls these "principal dangers." They are the risks in which the probability of occurrence and potential negative impact could undermine a grantee's ability to achieve the results. Equally important, the team explains how the grantee proposes to manage these "mortal" risks to success.

The upside-down risks: changing opportunities and dangers

Risk exposure to both positive and negative results must be managed into the future and this, of course, is the grantee's responsibility. The project proposal is essentially a plan for the management of the positive risks. The grantee informs Novib how it will manage the negative risks. Together, they agree on an agenda to monitor and review progress towards the results and the control of the principal dangers. This annual reflection analyzes how the opportunity and dangers may have changed, but also identifies new opportunities and emerging threats for the coming year. In sum, the content of the appraisal highlights the positive risks and the opportunity to contribute to significant social change. The negative risks are those that endanger success.

ENGAGEMENT AND DIALOGUE

Novib's grant appraisal methodology is based on mutual respect between Novib and its grantees and a sound understanding of each other's expectations and needs. A program officer and the officer's team quickly confirm a promising opportunity (and weed out others). They analyse only the important obstacles to success and make decisions using judgment and reflection, as well as facts and figures, all in consultation with the grantee. The risk appraisal enables Novib staff and grantees to negotiate agreements about enhancing the opportunity to cooperate and mitigating the dangers to the success of that cooperation.

The pre-assessment team meeting

First, Novib communicates to all applicants that Novib supports grantees that take risks in seizing new opportunities to achieve their social change goals. Upon receiving a project proposal, one team member, usually a program officer, decides or confirms in the case of a current grantee if the project proposal meets Novib's minimum criteria.

- Fits within Novib's grant-making strategy for the country or region.
- Is compatible in terms of organizational purpose and values.
- Fulfills minimum administrative and financial standards, such as being a legally constituted NGO organization with a bank account.

If the team agrees in principle to appraise the organization and its proposal, the program officer in the lead prepares a draft appraisal for discussion by her team with the information at hand. This includes the grantee's proposal and for current grantees, evaluations, annual reports, audits, and field visit notes. Experience to date is that key additional information is always required. For example, usually there is a lack of clarity about the intended results of the grantee's activities. In Novib's case, this is especially true concerning potential policy and practice changes. Of course, the use of a risk appraisal methodology also requires a change in mindset within the Novib team. For instance, the previous appraisal methodology was calibrated to identify problems and set conditions, not embrace positive and negative risks.

Visit to the grantee

Generally, not all the missing information can be obtained through correspondence. The customary emphasis by donors is on what the grantee is going to *do* with their grant. Novib's new focus on what is to be *achieved* and on the results represents a new dimension to the donor-grantee relationship and requires face-toface dialogue. Therefore, the team crafts the questions that one or two program officers, sometimes accompanied by the financial officer, pursue during the visit to the organization. They begin with a morning or afternoon of questions and answers to gather information. The grantee's director, senior management team, and board members, occasionally, are present.

In the following day or two, the program officer (and other team members if present) completes the draft appraisal and presents it to the grantee. The grantee reads and discusses internally the appraisal before another session with the program officer(s). In the second half-day meeting, it is the grantee's turn to ask questions, correct misinformation, and comment on the analysis in the risk appraisal. They wrap up discussing how the grantee will manage the negative risks.

The visit is the central event in the appraisal process. The face-to-face critical dialogue is sharply focused on the political dimension of the cooperation—what both NGOs aim to change in society. In the first year, Novib applied the risk appraisal methodology to project proposals from almost 200 NGOs in countries with a wide range of political, economic, and cultural diversity. Around the world, grantees and Novib staff alike consistently consider this respectful, transparent discussion in a spirit of conscious risk-taking and mutual accountability to be the most valuable part of the new methodology. They are able to counter together the pressures for donors to subcontract for results and for grantees to play cat and mouse in order to preserve their institutional integrity. Grantees learn why Novib is supporting (or not funding) a project, as well as Novib's hopes for and concerns about their projects. Novib learns about the fundamental challenges the NGO counterpart faces in achieving significant social change.

Team discussion and decision

The program officer responsible submits to the team the appraisal and a ten to twenty page description of the grantee. The two documents—one part analysis and the other part facts and figures—complement each other. The program officer has sifted through considerable amounts of information, has analysed that which is essential to understand the opportunity for cooperation, and made judgments about the impact and likelihood of both success and failure. All of this has been done in consultation with the NGO grantee. Therefore, the team does not repeat or simulate the process of appraisal. Instead, colleagues enrich the quality and coherence of both products.

In making their decision to fund, the team members go beyond examining the probability and the importance of potential structural, sustainable changes in the lives of people represented by the project to be funded. They strive together to strengthen, integrate, respect, and accept responsibility for Novib's and the grantee's necessarily different but convergent views.

Follow-up and review

The Novib methodology stipulates a review of the opportunities and dangers at least once a year. The grantee and program officer discuss the grantee's experience in the past twelve months in working towards achieving the results and managing the principal dangers and the implications for opportunities and dangers in the second year. The review also looks forward: How has the opportunity changed? Are there new opportunities that may deserve higher priority? How have the threats changed? What new action is required to manage them?

PARTICIPATORY MANAGEMENT FOR NGOS

The NGO management debate has attempted to address the question: what style of management is appropriate for NGOs? In so doing, the debate is valuable. However, given that participation in decision-making is a feature of governmental and commercial organisations, the association of a participatory style of management with a distinctive approach to NGO management is unhelpful.

It is more useful to examine the advantages of participation to organisations generally, and to NGOs in particular, and then identify those factors in the NGO context which make a participatory approach more appropriate for them. There are a number of perspectives on the increasing interest in participation in the commercial sector.

Guest and Knight (1979) argue that it represents part of the search for... a new means of overcoming industrial and economic problems, changing market conditions internationally, rising expectations of the workforce, and interest in the concept of industrial democracy. The emphasis on changing environmental conditions is taken up by Lawler (1986: 19) who insists that 'the societal, business, product, and work force changes that have occurred argue strongly for a change in management style', and who believes that 'in most situations some form of participative management is the best answer' (Lawler, 1986: 11). At the same time, Wall and Lischeron (1977: 1) point out that in contemporary society 'participation, in one form or another, is seen as one means of improving the quality of working life'. However, the increased interest in participation cannot simply be seen as stemming from changed contextual factors and a desire for greater work humanisation.

An instrumental view of participation-that greater participation will lead to greater efficiency, and consequently greater profits-is fundamental in the commercial sector, and is particularly reflected in the 'hard', rather than the 'soft' approach to Human Resource Management (Storey, 1987).8 That participation is linked to improved performance is evident from Ouchi (1981) who states: Decision-making by consensus has been the subject of a great deal of research in Europe and the United States over the past twenty years, and the evidence strongly suggests that a consensus approach yields more creative decisions and more effective implementation than does individual decision-making. Moreover, the participation of staff is inextricably linked with the concept of 'learning organisations'.

Senge (1990: 3), for example, argues that 'the organisations that will truly excel in the future will be the organisations that discover how to tap people's commitment and capacity to learn at all levels of an organisation'. 'Participatory management' and participatory development' As noted earlier, several authors argue that a participatory approach to management is particularly suitable for NGOs whose work involves the promotion of participation and the empowerment of beneficiaries. Chambers (1983: 210), for example, insists that such a management style is more in keeping with 'bottom-up development' or a participatory development approach. NGOs require a 'new professionalism' based on fundamental 'reversals' in the values, attitudes and behaviour of NGO staff, so that the people whom the NGO aims to support are truly empowered. Carroll's (1992: 205) study of NGOs in Latin America demonstrates that an open, collegial management style builds confidence and trust among beneficiaries and support organisations, and is, therefore, a key organisational quality for promoting popular participation. Similarly, the British Overseas Development Administration points out that 'culture, management structure, goals and sources of funding, all influence the manner and extent to which an aid agency can enhance the participation of other stakeholders'.

Indeed, Roche (1992: 188) argues: Experience suggests that a decentralised structure with semiautonomous, self-managed federated units, coupled with information and cooperative learning, is perhaps the most appropriate organisational design for supporting micro-development. A second theme that emerges in the literature is that NGOs need to develop decentralised and participatory decision-making structures, and adopt a problemsolving rather than a predictive blue-print approach to management, to ensure flexibility and maintain the ability to adapt to constantly changing realities. In particular, participatory planning processes are important as it is the field staff who normally have closest contact with beneficiaries (Sahley, 1995).

This 'effectiveness' argument is also taken up, for

example, by Brodhead and Herbert-Copley (1988), who suggest that NGOs must adopt a participatory approach in order to have wider impact. A third theme which emerges is the expectations of NGO staff. Clark (1991: 61), for example, states that: NGO staff are generally highly committed to their work because of widely shared values and a belief in the social change mission inherent in their work. This generates a sense of ownership which, when combined with the widespread expectation that organisations promoting democracy and participation should themselves be democratic, means that 'an autocratic style simply wouldn't work: the staff require participation'. Moreover, Hodson (1992: 135) argues that as NGOs grow 'decentralised and consensual forms of decision-making' are of particular importance 'if decisions are to be seen by staff as legitimate'.

In addition, there is an assumption that respect for workers leads to improved organisational functioning. Clark, (1991: 62), for example, suggests: Naturally an organisation of principled and committed workers will function best if staff feel respected, and listened to. The 'NGO management debate' cannot be easily resolved. In particular, a number of questions about the appropriateness of a participatory style of management for NGOs remain unanswered. Moreover, the debate about the appropriateness of 'participatory management' is constrained by a degree of definitional ambiguity which needs to be addressed.

NGO PARTNERSHIPS FOR GLOBAL HEALTH PROMOTION

The role of civil society organizations (CSOs) has received increasing importance in public policy and health policy over the past decade. As more financial and other resources were invested in this sector, the profile of its constituent groups changed. Different agencies define CSOs and NGOs differently. There is need for clarity in understanding the heterogeneity of this sector, and to recognize the unique roles of different constituents for global health promotion.

NGOs in the 1960s and 1970s were largely not –for – profit voluntary organizations working towards integral development. In health they included medical service through hospitals, health centres, and mobile clinics run by charities, missions and philanthropic organizations. With experience and reflection this group developed a deeper community based understanding of the dynamics of health, health care and development in different socio-cultural situations.

They were often able to achieve what governments in resource poor situations could not. With professional and social skills developed through working in difficult circumstances they became alternative experts, and the sector soon became an additional policy option. With growing recognition, money and influence, the profile of NGOs and new entrants to the sector changed. NGOs now include corporate NGOs, with companies setting up Trusts and Societies, building brand images, obtaining tax benefits and blurring the profit and not for profit sector. Government NGOs (GONGOs) and other new entities developed to overcome the bureaucracy of government. Professional associations' and research bodies with a high degree of knowledge and expertise, such as the International Union for Health Promotion and Education comprise another important section. NGO networks developed at national and global levels with a specific focus on health. During the past decade a global people's health movement emerged with a strong focus on health determinants and a right's based approach to health care. The potential for partnerships are thus many. Including those that can impact on health determinants provide a strategic option to global health promotion.

NGO coalitions for health promotion

The Millennium Development Goals (MDGs) provide a renewed framework for partnerships between governmental and nongovernmental organizations to create an environment conducive to development and elimination of poverty. Investment in health is critical for development and achievement of the MDGs. Through advocacy for healthy public policy, NGOs increase community health literacy and knowledge. NGOs with diverse structures and functions are the *sine quo non* in health promotion due to their grass roots presence and closeness with communities, which enables them to respond to people's health needs, concerns and aspirations.

NGOs understand that health is produced not just by hospitals and health professionals, but by individuals and families in the context of their daily lives and by influencing health determinants. NGOs are a positive force through direct health empowerment and action with people, as well as by working on the deeper issues. They apply the principles of health promotion including capacity development, knowledge transfer, community participation, empowerment, intersectoral collaboration, equity and advocacy for sustainable development.

The agenda for health promotion involves tackling multiple determinants of health. No single governmental or nongovernmental organization can deal with the multiplicity of issues. This is a sound rationale for NGOs to establish networks and alliances between themselves and with academia, governmental and other organizations to maximize their resources and achieve better outcomes. Partnerships provide an opportunity to make best use of the strengths and comparative advantage of each organization. However NGO coalitions do not occur by chance. To be effective partnerships must be planned, fostered and managed. Partnerships can be focused and time bound to achieve defined outcomes or work through long-term commitments. An example is the Geneva based NGO Ad Hoc Advisory Group on Health Promotion.

NGO Ad Hoc Advisory Group on Health Promotion

Born as an outcome of the WHO 4th International Conference on Health promotion in Jakarta in 1997, the Group supported implementation of its recommendations, and worked in partnership with others towards the Global Conference on Health Promotion in Mexico City, 2000.

The Group comprises several NGOs whose activities include health promotion and education, health co-operatives, nursing, rural women; social welfare, women's health and those whose main mandate may not be "health". Member's commitment to health promotion helps pool resources and expertise in tackling health determinants. For example, Associated County Women of the World (ACWW) partners with local NGOs, and Governments to provide literacy centres in Mali. ACWW provides partial funding and expertise to help local NGOs achieve their goals with community ownership and ongoing monitoring.

The wide diversity of activities, international structures and grass root involvement give the NGO Ad

Hoc Group its richness of approach, experience and expertise. Working collectively and individually, and in close partnership with WHO headquarters, the Group has kept the Jakarta and Mexico agendas in the forefront of the NGO community. The Group hosts briefings at the World Health Assembly on NGO and government partnerships in health promotion. This would not have been possible for any single NGO. By their work and commitment, the Ad Hoc Group contributes to the attainment of the Millennium Development Goals.

Capacity Building

Human resources are the lynchpin to achieve health and development goals. Distortions in health care priorities hinder progress in health promotion. Major distortions include concentration of health facilities and personnel on urban populations rather than rural, on tertiary care rather than primary, on curative care rather than on promotive and preventative services and on the middle-class and better off rather than on the poor. Though the primary health care strategy promoted by WHO was designed to achieve greater equity and universal coverage, health reform and economically driven models of care reduced public spending on health and social services leading to growing inequities.

Besides misallocation and mal-distribution of resources, access to health care is hampered by shortage of competent health professionals capable of providing comprehensive health care. Poor investment in training, recruitment and retention, force health care workers to look for 'greener pastures' leading to brain drain. Nurses and physicians trained at public cost migrate from poorer countries to the developed world, leaving health care facilities in a state of collapse.

Nursing staff shortages cause closure of essential health care facilities, including emergency rooms. Serious shortages in all health professional categories in Zimbabwe resulted in closure of health facilities and reduced access to services. The New York Times reported, "*the nation is currently engulfed in a huge nursing shortage which is going to get worse*". In the United Kingdom there is concern that: "*the National Health Service (NHS) does not have enough pairs of hands to deliver the care that the nation needs... and hospitals are turning abroad to find staff*"

Shortages of doctors are reported in several countries including Botswana, Ghana and Guinea Bissau. In some developing countries, shortage of nurses and doctors often results in staffing rural clinics by poorly trained personnel ill-equipped to provide comprehensive services including health promotion. In these circumstances, it is likely that investment in health promotion will continue to be eroded and neglected. NGO coalitions and all stakeholders need to address this issue on priority.

Health promotion strategies draw upon multiple actors and stakeholders including multilateral organizations such as UN agencies; development banks; national and local governments; faith-based groups, citizen's organizations; international, national and local NGOs; WHO collaborating centres; academic institutions; trade unions; the arts and entertainment industry; the private sector and others. Collaborative efforts by stakeholders who promote the public good in health is crucial for success. For example, the progress made in onchocerciacis control was only possible with committed partnerships. While reducing under-nutrition and universalizing access to water and sanitation attract less attention, regressive policies of some organizations also reverse health gains.

Community Empowerment

Different stakeholders, working with empowered communities can become a powerful voice, lobbying governments to invest in human resources particularly for health promotion training and capacity building. NGO networks have a convening power and a large outreach capacity enabling them to bring about a "paradigm shift" from the curative to the preventive, promotive and social health model. Training and capacity building by NGOs are characterized by active community participation, empowering individuals and families to increase control over the determinants of their health, and to demand universal access to health care. NGOs and health profession associations should be enabled to become "social health activists".

Coalition building

Strengthening NGO coalitions for health is necessary in the current landscape characterized by declining development resources, increasing privatization of services, and reverse transfer of resources from developing countries. Coalitions need to be built with skill, care and mutual trust using strategies that include identifying opportunities and partners with shared goals; reaching agreements; maintaining and evaluating partnerships. This takes time and resources.

Challenges faced include selecting partners, working with communities, defining partnerships goals, setting time frames, mobilising resources and keeping long term commitments to meet complex evolving needs. Often unequal distribution of power and decision-making within NGO groups or between NGOs and governments can negatively impact outcomes and sustainability of partnerships. Corporate interests working through governments and international bodies can be counterproductive. Lack of trust and suspicion between NGOs and governments is a potential threat.

Coalitions can multiply actions outlined in the Ottawa Charter: building healthy public policy, creating supportive environments, strengthening community action, developing personal skills, and reorienting health services. Mutual commitments to engagement between governments, civil society and NGOs would help achieve better health. Governments need to see beyond their term in office and to see the long-term role of health promotion. NGOs and civil society need to be rooted in their reality, and to see beyond that reality and their own constituencies to engage with a wider spectrum of stakeholders. Both need to recognize barriers that prevent the realization of health promotion in the community and to undertake cooperative measures to tackle this. As an intergovernmental agency, WHO has a long history of working with NGOs In health promotion WHO – NGO partnership from decision making to evaluation has been fruitful. While partnerships are strong at WHO headquarters, there is scope for improvement at country and regional levels.

GLOBAL COALITION'S PROMOTING HEALTH, ADDRESSING DETERMINANTS

Concern about the social determinants of health, and the difficulties faced by governments and international bodies to effectively work on their own towards Health for All goals, resulted in the emergence in the late 1990s of a much broader global coalition, the Peoples Health Movement (PHM). Unlike the 1970s, health groups and

NGOs are now joined by women's movements, the science and literacy movement, the environment movement, trade unions, development groups and many community based organizations, all of whom recognize that better health is a common concern.

Collective analysis, planning, action and reflections with affected communities build solidarity. Groups from varied backgrounds and cultures have become connected locally and globally through horizontal and vertical linkages. This awakening culminated in the first Peoples Health Assembly (PHA 1) in December 2000 in Savar, Bangladesh, wherein 1493 persons from 75 countries debated health related issues over five days and adopted the Peoples Charter for Health.

Through thousands of prior community, village and town meetings, the Charter built on perspectives of people, whose voices are rarely heard. It clearly addresses health determinants, namely:

a) economic challenges posed by the global trading system, third world debt, intellectual property laws, speculative international capital flows;

b) social and political challenges, including the right to work and livelihood, gender issues, rights of expression, political participation and religious choice, the weakening of public institutions and services;

c) environmental challenges including water and air pollution, climate change, ozone layer depletion, nuclear energy and waste, toxic chemicals and pesticides, loss of bio-diversity, deforestation and soil erosion ;

d) war, violence, conflict and natural disasters.

Action points concerning these issues, and for developing a people-centred health sector with people's participation resulted in much follow up. Spontaneously translated into 50 languages the Charter has become one of the largest consensus documents on health providing a framework for action. Since 2000, country, regional and issue based circles evolved leading to specific action such as the right to health care campaign in India; advocacy regarding global public private initiatives; policy dialogue with the WHO; a global campaign on patents; the Peoples Charter on HIV/AIDS and Asian People's Alliance for Combating HIV/AIDS; the first Global Health Watch report; International Health Forums; state national and UNESCAP health policies; a Tsunami Watch; and most importantly advocacy, street action and community work, including training thousands of community health workers. Media strategies resulted in greater national and local reporting of health issues and controversies, including corruption. In some countries health moved higher on the public and political agenda with commitments to increase budgetary allocations. There has been support for the peace movement in the USA, Europe and Asia, and a PHM response to disasters in Iran, Sri Lanka, and India. The second Peoples Health Assembly in Cuenca, Ecuador in July 2005 raised issues and concerns of the Americas and reviewed progress since PHA I.

8

Global Governance

Explaining and understanding global governance requires interpretation. Interpretation, in turn, takes place within a theoretical framework. As global governance is a multi-faceted process, the study of it requires a theoretical framework that goes beyond a single paradigm. I will, therefore, employ a pluralist approach that is informed by insights gained mainly, but not exclusively, from realist, liberal, and constructivist research programmes. My task is complicated by the fact that there are several variants of realism, liberalism, and constructivism. Moreover, even when taken together, these three paradigms cannot shed light on every facet of global life. I have chosen them because they go a long way toward explaining power, order, norms, and change. As Stephen Walt has argued: "The 'complete diplomat' of the future should remain cognizant of realism's emphasis on the inescapable role of power, keep liberalism's awareness of domestic forces in mind, and occasionally reflect on constructivism's vision of change."

Realist accounts of global politics tend to emphasize the way in which states use power to maximise their national interests. They posit that the most important international actors are sovereign states, which are rational and operate in an inherently competitive, anarchic, and self-help environment. Realists assume that sovereignty makes states functionally similar. They also emphasize the strategies that states devise in efforts to improve their standing in international economic competition, influence weaker states, or compete for international prestige.

Thus, realists focus on military balancing and "positional competition" in economic, technological, and other non-military matters. They acknowledge the existence of globalization, civil society, and transnational forces, but they make no room for them in their analyses. While realism may be helpful in highlighting the role of power and self-interest in global governance, it discounts the function of ideas, culture, institutions, and norms, except as instruments in power politics.

At a glance, liberalism would appear to be the most appropriate approach to use in the study of global governance because, as Michael Doyle has observed, it is identified "with an essential principle, the importance of the freedom of the individual." Liberalism can adequately explain the interactions of states, civil society, MNCs, and IGOs in global governance.

The liberal perspective on global politics posits that there "is at the minimum a heterogeneous state of peace and war" which could "become a state of global peace, in which the expectation of war disappears." Liberals believe that IGOs, such as the United Nations, play a vital role in world politics. They acknowledge that "states live under international anarchy," but they argue that "states are inherently respectful of international law" and that they "do not experience a general state of war." Liberals reject the realist claim that states are functionally similar units. Doyle, for example, has argued that states "are inherently different units", differentiated by how they relate to individual human rights. In general, liberals believe that the interests of states extend beyond security and include the protection of human rights.

Constructivism is concerned with the way in which norms, rules, and institutions constitute the identities and interests of states and other international actors. It claims that the structures of human association, including international society, are determined primarily by shared ideas and culture rather than material forces.

While realists claim that it is the distribution of capabilities that determines the nature of the international system, constructivists argue that those capabilities have meaning only because of the ideas we attach to them. Constructivists claim that it is the distribution of ideas and culture that determines the shape of the international system. As constructivism focuses on the roles of norms, ideas, and culture in constructing international structures, it would have plenty to say about how global governance is constituted.

As already indicated, global governance is about norms and power. It consists of ideas, culture, and material forces. It also helps generate norms, ideas, and culture. Global governance involves states and non-state actors, and it affects life from the local to the global levels.

However, it is the theoretical frameworks utilized to understand it that determine the way norms and power are interpreted. It is for this reason that I have elected to employ a pluralist theoretical approach.

THE INTERPRETIVE COMMUNITY AND GLOBAL GOVERNANCE

Global governance, which is essentially a product of liberal thinking, concerns so-called global values, norms, standards, and rules. The majority of values that are considered global are Western, and so global governance basically facilitates, and reflects, Western hegemony. Western hegemony here refers to the dominance of Western institutions, interests, standards, and NGOs. The "global civil society" is based on Western mores. In global governance, non-Western states and NGOs have had to redefine their interests and identities in relation to Western norms and power. Severe socio-economic problems have delivered developing nation political leaders and NGOs into the hands of the West, thereby making Western hegemony appear like an "empire by invitation."

The dominance of Western institutions is partly due to the function of an "interpretive community" that constantly explains, promotes, advocates, and justifies global governance. The "interpretive community" has been extremely successful in portraying Western ideas, values, and preferences as global. The term "interpretive community" is used in this chapter to refer to any group of people who are committed to providing justification and legitimating principles for particular institutions, values, or practices. Members of an "interpretive community" may come from different professional backgrounds; they may be scholars, journalists, international civil servants, and NGO workers. They may also be recruited from different countries and might not even be aware that they operate as a part of a global "interpretive community." What they have in common is a conviction that they are interpreting reality, when in fact they may only be expressing aspirations. Sometimes the ideas of an "interpretive community" may influence practice.

In the post-Cold War era, members of a global "interpretive community" have converged on several themes, including a new world order, globalization, and new forms of sovereignty and security. For example, in December 1988, Soviet President Mikhail Gorbachev used the phrase "new world order" in his address to the United Nations to underline the new strategic thinking and the global restructuring he envisaged, but the "world" simply ignored it. However, when US President George Bush used the same phrase two years later, the "world" took notice. In condemning Iraq's invasion of Kuwait in August 1990, Bush talked of a new world order "where the rule of law supplants the rule of the jungle, a world in which nations recognize the shared responsibility for freedom and justice." This liberal aspiration contrasted sharply with the realist logic of power politics, in which war between state is always considered a possibility. It was no more than a wish for a different type of international system in the post-Cold War era, but other world leaders, scholars, and journalists subsequently started talking of a new world order as if it were a reality. Bush's aspiration did not spell an end to power politics; instead it gave impetus to a rethinking of norms in world politics, and this, in turn, energized efforts to portray Western values, standards, and institutions as global norms.

It was in this intellectual climate that the Commission on Global Governance issued a report which defined sovereignty as an institution that is ultimately derived from the people: "It is a power to be exercised by, for, and on behalf of the people of a state." This report implies that sovereignty should be respected only if the people of a state have had an opportunity to exercise their political, economic, and cultural rights. The report also argues that "the principle of sovereignty and the norms that derive from it must be further adapted to recognize changing realities." Further-more, "global security extends beyond the protection of borders, ruling elites, and exclusive state interests to include the protection of people." The Commission was simply expressing aspirations that may become practice one day.

At about the same time, a former Australian foreign minister, Gareth Evans, argued that the concept of security, "as it appears in the [UN] Charter, is as much about the protection of individuals as it is about the defence of the territorial integrity of states." In April 1991, former UN Secretary-General Javier Perez de Cuellar had argued that state sovereignty needed to be reassessed in response to "the shift in public attitudes towards the belief that the defence of the oppressed in the name of morality should prevail over frontiers and legal documents." Similarly, his successor, Boutros Boutros-Ghali, argued that the time of absolute and exclusive sovereignty had passed. The current UN Secretary-General, Kofi Annan, went further in redefining sovereignty, when he told the General Assembly in September 1999 that his interpretation of the UN Charter was that it aims "to protect individual human beings, not to protect those who abuse them." Annan argued, in his speech to the General Assembly in 1999, that sovereignty had been "redefined by the forces of globalization and international cooperation," and that the state was the "servant of its people, and not *vice versa*."

The conclusions of the Commission on Global

Governance and those of UN secretaries-general and other analysts in recent years suggest that the rethinking of norms has given rise to an interpretive community which is ready to argue for changes in the practices of sovereignty. By arguing for liberal interpretations of the UN Charter, they have promoted a particular view of global governance. However, the views of an interpretive community, without changes in the practices of the majority of international actors, cannot constitute a shift in the meaning of sovereignty. According to some analysts, it was not possible in the 1990s to see a clear-cut turn in state practices. As Adam Roberts has observed, while idealists have hoped that "the sovereignty of states would take second place to human rights," humanitarian action in the 1990s "owed much to political considerations that were often tinged with an element of *realpolitik*".

It is such interpretations that set the stage on which "NGOs and... IGOs grope, sometimes cooperatively, sometimes competitively, sometimes in parallel, towards a modicum of global governance." What these interpretations do not say is that global governance links together "global civil society," individuals, the state, and market forces. It is also about the generation of, and the response to, "shared" values and institutions, which give rise to processes for identifying issues, forming an agenda, arriving at outcomes, and making arrangements to implement them. However, as the preceding paragraphs show, global governance has definite implications for interpretations of sovereignty.

SOVEREIGNTY AND GLOBAL GOVERNANCE

State sovereignty is like a living organism; it casts off its meanings as it evolves in response to the demands of global governance. In simple terms, sovereignty can be described as a principle that legitimizes internal political organization and serves as a mechanism for enhancing international order. It is, therefore, linked to both internal and global governance. As Thomas Biersteker and Cynthia Weber have argued, state sovereignty is "a political entity's externally recognized right to exercise final authority over its affairs." With regard to internal political control, sovereignty revolves around population, territory, and recognized authority. Alan James has added a constitutional dimension to this, claiming that "sovereign states are those territorially-based entities which are independent in terms of their constitutional arrangements".

For the purposes of this chapter, I shall distinguish between three types of sovereignty. The first is external or juridical sovereignty, which is based on the notion that, theoretically, "the state has over it no other authority than that of international law." The second is internal or empirical sovereignty, which is based on the view that states have the right (and capacity) to control the people, resources, and institutions within their territories. The third is individual or popular sovereignty, which is predicated on the claim that all people are entitled to fundamental freedoms and that states exercise control over them only with their consent. Empirical sovereignty and juridical sovereignty accord states rights and responsibilities that other international actors do not have.

The concept of global governance implicitly questions some understandings of sovereignty because it is based on the assumption that states and non-state actors are partners in the management of global affairs. Realists, who claim that states are the most important international actors, would regard global governance as a diminution of sovereignty. The realist view of sovereignty is that theoretically each state is free to pursue its domestic and external affairs without outside interference. Hence Hans Morgenthau's definition of sovereignty as "centralized power that exercised its law-making-and law-enforcing authority within a certain territory." On the other hand, liberals, who subscribe to the view that transnational forces play important roles in world politics, regard global governance as a necessary process of addressing anarchy in the absence of central authority. Liberals believe that sovereignty gives states the right to exercise control within their territories, but that this control is to be exercised with some degree of consent and legitimacy from society. For this reason, liberals associate empirical sovereignty with popular sovereignty. Constructivists, who consider sovereignty to be socially constructed, regard global governance as a part of the social construction and reconstruction of international society.

A closer examination of the different perceptions of sovereignty will shed more light. The realist perspective of sovereignty, which is state-centric and absolutist, is often traced back to Jean Bodin in the fifteenth century. Bodin defined sovereignty as "the absolute and perpetual power" of the ruler. Later, Thomas Hobbes elaborated similar views in his *Leviathan.* Both perceptions of sovereignty reflected the overriding concern for order and security in France and England, respectively. As Alexander Murphy has argued, Bodin's main concern was to promote peace. Endorsing Bodin and Hobbes, Hinsley has argued that sovereignty refers to "a final and absolute political authority in the political community." Some writers have continued to view sovereignty from this perspective alone, thereby entrenching the realist viewpoint. However, Hinsley and many others have argued that in practice there have been limitations to the exercise of sovereignty, with Hinsley observing that sovereignty is not a fact but a concept of how political power is exercised. This state-centric perspective is a normative position that originated from absolutist Europe. Indeed, Reus-Smit has argued that the moral purpose of the state in absolutist Europe was to preserve a "divinely ordained" and hierarchical order, and this gave rise to an authoritative norm of procedural justice.

The liberal view of sovereignty may be traced back to John Locke and Thomas Paine. Paine, for example, associated popular sovereignty with international peace. In reference to the American Revolution in 1791, he argued: "Monarchical sovereignty, the enemy of mankind, and the source of misery, is abolished; and sovereignty is restored to its natural and original place, the nation... Were this the case throughout Europe, the cause of war would be taken away." Locke's ideas, which defined sovereignty in relation to the consent of individuals and civil society, were also consistent with liberal democracy. In the early twentieth century, liberal scholars, who were opposed to the Austinian juristic theory of the state, defined sovereignty in terms of people's rights. For example, Harold Laski claimed that sovereignty belonged to the people. In recent times, some liberals have argued that transnational forces and NGOs have a legitimate role in world politics, and that sovereignty should not stand in their way. The liberal perspective on sovereignty readily accommodates the norms, power structures, and regulatory mechanisms that underpin global governance.

Constructivists have had a lot to say about sovereignty

in the past decade. Indeed, some of the severest critics of our knowledge of sovereignty have been constructivists and critical theorists. Rob Walker, for instance, recognizes sovereignty as "the primary constitutive principle of modern political life," but he argues that its history has not been properly explained and suggests that it is necessary "to be wary of the conventional history of... state sovereignty." Constructivists are critical of those who treat sovereignty as an unchanging institution. Reus-Smit, for example, has argued that it is the constitutional structures of society that determine the nature of sovereignty. The norms that underpin global governance are part of these constitutional structures.

The assumptions that underpin sovereignty date back to the Peace of Westphalia, which inaugurated a new "international" legal order for Europe. The Westphalian regime, which brought about a break from the previous religious order, is best remembered for making the territorial state the cornerstone of the modern international system. Since then, the development and reinterpretation of sovereignty have closely mirrored the evolution of the state and the prevailing norms of global governance. However, sovereignty has not always been honoured. In Europe, sovereignty was occasionally subverted with a view to maintaining the balance of power. This is partly why Stephen Krasner has claimed that breaches of the Westphalian model "have been an enduring characteristic of the international environment. Krasner has more recently written of sovereignty as "organized hypocrisy." Others have suggested that sovereignty can be understood only with reference to particular historical periods.

Sovereignty has undergone various transformations

in accordance with the prevailing norms of global governance. Whenever serious crises undermine the legitimizing principles of sovereignty, new norms are negotiated, and these norms often reflect the preferences of the hegemonic states. It is the processes of negotiating the rules for sovereignty which Biersteker and Weber had in mind when they argued that sovereignty was socially constructed. They posited that it is "the practices of states and non-state agents [that] produce, reform, and redefine sovereignty and its constitutive elements." In such social interactions, all participants help to shape, and are also shaped by, the structure of the system, in varying degrees. A global structure that is characterized by power politics and secret diplomacy is likely to favour the notion that sovereignty resides with governments. However, a global order which is committed to the promotion of democracy and human rights would favour popular sovereignty. Thus, it is the norms, values, and institutions which underpin global governance that determine the nature of sovereignty.

Westphalian sovereignty was perceived to reside with political leaders and governments. Under this system, the defence of sovereignty provided governments with an excuse to impose dictatorial rule. This autocratic sovereignty was undermined first by the 1776 American revolution, with its emphasis on popular sovereignty, and then by the 1789 French revolution, with its ideas of equality, fraternity, and liberty. After the Napoleonic wars, the Vienna Congress in 1815 was hostile to populist ideas and legitimized neo-Westphalian sovereignty based on monarchical control. This changed after World War 1, when the 1919 Versailles Conference legitimized sovereignty based on the nationalist norm. However, this norm did not apply to African and Asian political entities, which had become subject to European colonialism. Thus, in its evolution, sovereignty has oscillated between governmental "proprietorship" and popular "possession."

Sovereignty has closely been identified with territory for more than 350 years, but the inviolability of territorial integrity and the non-intervention norm were given more emphasis at the end of World War II. This extra emphasis privileged the state over its people. The Cold War, which, in Alexander Wendt's words, "was a structure of shared knowledge that governed great power relations," ensured that this state-centric interpretation of sovereignty reigned supreme. During this period, recognition of new states was determined by whether or not they were ready to respect the non-intervention norm and to uphold juridical sovereignty. Popular sovereignty and good governance had no room in this scheme, partly because the two superpowers-the United States and the Soviet Union—could not agree on what form of internal governance was desirable. With the end of the Cold War, Western powers have emphasized normative values and empirical sovereignty, and this has given the impression that sovereignty is increasingly being associated with the democratic norm. However, the emphasis which the Western states and international financial institutions have placed on liberal democracy and Popular legitimacy appears to be geared towards consolidating Western hegemony. The processes of globalization have facilitated this.

GLOBALIZATION AND GLOBAL GOVERNANCE

Global governance and globalization have a chicken-egg relationship. One is said to be a cause, or product, of the other. This chapter will not engage in the argument as to whether globalization precedes global governance or *vice versa*. Neither of them can be traced to a specific date. What is clear is that globalization has become one of the most commonly used terms in international relations, although (or because) its meaning remains imprecise. Jan Aart Scholte has argued that globalization "refers to processes whereby social relations acquire relatively distanceless and borderless qualities." This is a useful starting point, but it does not say much about the globalization processes themselves. As with many social phenomena, the theoretical framework in play determines the meaning attached to globalization.

Realists, for example, do not think much of globalization because of the importance they attach to the state and national interests. To them, globalization is basically a product of "positional competition" by states, in their efforts to gain advantage in non-military sectors. For some developing nation' analysts, globalization is a form of westernization and colonization that can be traced back several centuries. They perceive it in terms of the domination of the non-industrial world by industrialized countries. The market-orientated liberals, on the other hand, have defined globalization primarily in terms of the contemporary movement of capital, investment, and other economic interactions, thereby equating it with economic interdependence. They sometimes regard globalization as the hidden force behind economic cooperation, financial markets, and free trade rules. Thus, the establishment of the World Trade Organization in the mid-1990s was a major development in global governance. Hurrell and Woods summed up the liberal perspective, in which globalization is a "process of increasing interdependence and global enmeshment-which occurs as money, people, images, values, and ideas flow ever more swiftly and smoothly across national boundaries." The "flow" of people across state borders has to be qualified, as most developed countries have restricted the entry of developing world peoples. For constructivists, globalization is a part of the global structure that constitutes the identities and interests of international actors and is, in turn, constituted by the interactions of these actors.

In this chapter, the term " globalization" is used to describe the intensity and breadth of interactions within the political, technological, economic, social, and cultural domains, most of which are derived from Western, and especially capitalist, values and practices. Due to improvements in information technology, globalization partly refers to the processes through which social, political, and economic relations can be conducted instantaneously throughout the world and may sometimes elude state attempts at restriction. In a globalized world, political, cultural, economic, and social events tend to become more interconnected. The emphasis is on the size, depth, and speed of interactions.

Globalization implies universalization, harmonization, and homogeneity, which ultimately means that the values, institutions, interests, and norms of some peoples and societies have to be sacrificed. To the extent that globalization implies the promotion of values and standards derived from the West, it inevitably poses a threat to the existence of non-Western traditions and institutions. The threat that globalization poses to developing world peoples is not only more severe but also of a different type from that which it presents to those of the developed, global north.

While some liberals have suggested that globalization has eclipsed the state both within its territory and internationally, realists argue that globalization has in fact been created and maintained by states. As Ian Clark has observed, globalization could be seen as a symptom of "wider Political and economic policies" and as "the product of specific state policy choices." There is no doubt that globalization has had some effects on state behaviour. Rapid changes in the technology of transport and communications have made it necessary for policy-makers to devise new ways of responding to both domestic and global problems. In this sense, globalization is a restructuring process that cannot be ignored by policy makers. However, states, especially the great powers, still determine the environment in which other international actors operate. For example, it was the developed countries that organized financial rescue plans for Indonesia, South Korea, and Thailand in 1997. It is partly for this reason that some have argued that globalization is directed by states' policies.

Explaining how globalization relates to global governance requires a reiteration of my earlier discussion of sovereignty. Sovereignty not only defines the identities and capabilities of groups in world politics, but also limits the ability of outsiders to interfere in domestic affairs. Thus, sovereignty determines agency or the capacity for independent action in world politics. In this sense, sovereignty and self-determination are interrelated. Self-determination provides a theory to explain when state boundaries are legitimate and when they are not, thus implying guidelines to use for deciding whether they should be honoured or not. The pursuit of self-determination legitimizes sovereignty. As with sovereignty, what self-determination involves has changed over time. A monarch could, literally, claim that his military capacities presented a *fait accompli* without worrying too much about whether he had the right to rule; he was, materially, self-determining. The French and American revolutions challenged this position and spread the notion that sovereignty ought to be popular. Then, the twentieth century produced two competing norms regarding "who" the "self" is in self-determination, each norm embodied in an international treaty. The Treaty of Versailles promoted ethnic self-determination and thereby legitimated sovereignty based on the nationalist norm. However, later international treaties, including the charters of the United Nations and the Organization of African Unity, promoted state self-determination, thereby legitimating sovereignty based largely on the territorial norm. What these conceptions shared was the idea that a group ought to be able to determine its own future, and that sovereignty was necessary to enable true autonomy.

With globalization, the interpretation of sovereignty and state capacity for independent action in world politics has been affected by two factors. Firstly, values which are associated with the West have been universalized and depoliticized. This has made possible the second factor, namely the change in international norms relating to development trajectories. There are no longer alternative paths to successful development. Modernization theory, discarded decades earlier, has made a comeback. Societies are arrayed on a single line: successful, civic, progressive, and Western at one end; failed, ethnic, primitive, and non-Western at the other. This has delegitimized political life outside the West, making intervention in non-Western states acceptable.

Globalization has prompted observers to claim that the Earth has become a global village. However, if the

Earth is a global village, it is one where only some inhabitants retain their traditions, cultures, rituals, and symbols. Western-derived rules and standards have constructed the so called global village. The interests and values of non-Westerners are largely ignored, except as tourist attractions.

The "global" values which are trumpeted under the banner of globalization were not arrived at through reflection and consensus in international society. They are the norms, symbols, and standards that have been promoted by the powerful Western countries, largely for their own benefit. Non-state actors, and especially NGOs, concerned with numerous problems such as human rights abuses, poverty, environmental degradation, and weapons of mass destruction have facilitated the promotion of Western values in the developing world.

It is no wonder that, as the forces for harmonization and universalization grow, non-Western peoples and their communities are striving to preserve control over local identities, symbols, and values. Thus localization, nationalism, and ethnic and religious revivalism have assumed significance partly because of the threat which universalization and harmonization pose to different cultures, standards, and interests.

These defensive reactions by non-Westerners to some aspects of globalization do not suggest that their identities and interests have always remained stagnant. They merely signal that the globalizing processes involved are too enormous and happen too fast. Indeed, it is partly through the speed of its challenge to diversity and identity that globalization constitutes a threat to the security of developing world peoples. It is perhaps for this reason that UN Deputy Secretary-General Louise Frechette has argued that globalization brings uncertainties in which "there are losers as well as winners." She touched on the nerve of globalization's contradictions when she observed that "globalization confronts us with the challenge of reconciling the imperatives of global markets with the socio-economic needs of the world's people; and of realising its full potential while minimizing the threat of new divisions in our world, of backlash and recourse to the damaging 'isms'... populism, nationalism, ethnic chauvinism, fanaticism, and terrorism."

The non-Western peoples and communities view globalization as a cause of alienation; they feel apathetic, detached, socially dislocated, powerless, and normless in the face of globalization. They are apathetic because they see themselves as outsiders in the global village. They also feel that the globalization processes have cast them aside. Alienation undermines what has been described as human security. In this instance, it results from the differences in power, opportunities, and advantages between the Western and non-Western societies.

Recent attempts to assert "Asian values" are partly a reaction to globalization. There is no consensus among the people of Asia as to what constitutes "Asian values," but it is a label with which some political leaders seek to legitimize certain forms of internal political order. Political leaders who seek to maintain authoritarianism and contain the opposition within their societies have exploited "Asian values."

These leaders may be believed by sections of the population, especially when they argue that their goal is to preserve Asian traditions in the face of the globalization juggernaut. Similarly, Islamic resurgence can be explained partly in terms of efforts by some Muslim groups to prevent the total erosion of their cultures. Occasionally, radical groups have used the cover of this resurgence to engage in political violence.

For example, the establishment of the Hezbollah in Lebanon's Bekaa Valley by Iranian zealots in the early 1980s, was partly based on the fact that the Shia Muslims in Lebanon were treated as second-class citizens, both economically and politically. But, Hezbollah was funded by the Iranian regime as part of its efforts to promote its own brand of Islam and to reshape the Middle Eastern regional order. The result was insecurity for foreigners in Lebanon, and hostage seizures.

However, it is not only non-Western peoples that fear the impact of globalization on their interests. French government officials have expressed serious concerns about the relationship between free trade and culture, particularly with regard to trade in audio-visual products. France was among several European countries that criticized aspects of the 1993 GATT agreement because of its potential impact on French culture and identity. Canadians have struggled with the potential of imported books and periodicals to edge out Canadian content, and have experimented with laws that establish excise tax or minimum quotas for Canadian content. And many of the most powerful Western countries, the engines behind globalization, re-enact the same confrontation domestically with immigrants.

Even with the enormous power asymmetry intact, some local French, Americans, Germans, and Australians, for example, fret publicly over the "threat" that immigrants supposedly pose to their culture. Nevertheless, the West as a whole celebrates globalization.

THE UNITED NATIONS AND THE FUTURE OF GLOBAL GOVERNANCE

Globalization and global governance will go on with or without the United Nations. Global governance has so far reflected mainly the interests of Western societies, but the United Nations has the potential to make it truly global. It has the potentiality to ensure that the ideas, norms, and rules which underpin global governance reflect the diversity of values and interests in the world. The United Nations needs to work out its programmes in such a way that racial, gender, cultural, and economic inequalities are taken into account wherever possible. Deputy Secretary General Frechette has emphasized three broad imperatives for the United Nations: legitimacy, instruments and institutions, and effectiveness. These are very important factors, but they are more complex than they first appear. This is because the United Nations means different things to various groups. In the remaining part of this chapter, I will briefly look at how realists, liberals, and constructivists view the legitimacy of the United Nations, and I will suggest finally that UN "managers" need to reinterpret the Charter consistently,

The United Nations appears to straddle the borderline between realism and liberalism, and it has lasted this long partly because it has been perceived by both realists and liberals to be in each of their own interests. Realists care about the legitimacy of the United Nations, but for them this legitimacy is derived from the United Nations serving as an instrument of state interests. A United Nations without the potentiality to serve as a device through which states use their power to pursue national interests has little legitimacy for the realists. There is no doubt that sections of the United Nations, especially the

Security Council, serve as a platform for power politics. What generally concerns developing world states is that most of the power within the United Nations is held by Western countries, which dominate the international system politically, economically, technologically, and militarily. Western countries also have the means to promote their values and norms more effectively than the non-Western states. That is why Samuel Huntington has argued: "The West in effect is using international institutions, military power, and economic resources to run the world in ways that will maintain Western predominance, protect Western interests, and promote Western political and economic values." Other realist scholars have made similar claims in relation to the Western states' control of the United Nations and other international organizations. For example, John Mearsheimer has argued: "The most powerful states in the system create and shape institutions so that they can maintain their share of world power, or even increase it. If the United Nations is to remain acceptable to the majority of people around the world, it has to erase the perception that it serves as a mechanism through which the values of powerful states are imposed on weaker ones.

If realists have been mainly interested in the exercising of power and the pursuit of national interests, liberals have been interested in the United Nations' universalist and progressive character. Liberals believe that the United Nations has Put Power Politics in check and facilitated the collective management of global public goods. From some liberal perspectives, the United Nations derives legitimacy from its inclusiveness and its potential to bring about human progress. As Ramesh Thakur has argued:' "The greatest strength of the United Nations is that it is the Only universal forum for international cooperation and management. It must continue to play a central role in establishing a normative order which strikes a balance between the competing demands of equity and political reality."

On the issues of democratization and participation, some liberals have argued that the United Nations has neglected non-state actors for too long. Hence the increasing calls for the United Nations to involve the "global civil society" more deeply in global governance. There is no doubt that a good number of NGOs have achieved phenomenal success in specific issue areas. However, agreeing on a mechanism for their participation with the United Nations in global governance is likely to raise difficult questions. NGOs have the capacity to do a great deal, but they have no obligation to do anything. Voluntary organizations are not accountable, even in theory, to those whom they serve. The United Nations requires great ingenuity to pursue democratization without compromising the effectiveness and universal acceptability of its actions.

For constructivists, the legitimacy of the United Nations is derived largely from its constitutive and transformative character. The United Nations is both a product, and producer, of ideas, norms, and state interests and identities. The world's leading constructivist in the international relations discipline, John Ruggie, is a senior adviser to the United Nations Secretary-General. Ruggie has said his transition from academia to the UN "went surprisingly smoothly because it quickly became apparent that creative leadership in international organization is social constructivism in action." The United Nations has been an agent of transformation. It has generated numerous ideas on such issues as development, the environment, human rights, women's rights, and peace-keeping. In this respect, the United Nations has become a very important norm-setting organization. As the interests, preferences, and identities of Member States are neither fixed nor exogenously given, the United Nations has participated, however marginally, in influencing the way they are defined and redefined.

However, there is a perception in the developing world that the United Nations' transformative power has been harnessed by the West and works to the detriment of non-Western interests. Some of these criticisms came out at the 1993 UN conference on human rights in Vienna, where China and developing countries described the universalization of human rights as a conspiracy by Western governments to pressure non-Western states to change their identities and political and economic systems.

However, the Vienna Declaration and Programme of Action achieved a classic compromise by stating that human rights are universal, indivisible, interdependent, and interrelated, while also recognising "the significance of national and regional particularities and various historical, cultural, and religious backgrounds."

The Vienna Declaration underscored the clash of two principles-universalism and relativism. Western countries and NGOs from both the north and the south supported the universalist perspective, while non-Western states took the relativist line. The conference also underlined the imperative for the United Nations to devise a formula through which its ideas and norms in the future will reflect the diversity of the global village.

The exigencies of global governance in this millennium require the United Nations to rethink its norms, structures, procedures, and practices. If the United Nations were to make a difference to global governance, it would need to address more seriously the imperative for democratization in its agencies, taking account of growing demands for transparency and popular participation.

Greater openness cannot be achieved without creative efforts to recast sovereignty. Thakur has argued in the introduction of this volume that the "Partial erosion of the... principle of national sovereignty is rooted today in the reality of global interdependence," but there is a general perception that this "erosion" is too slow and too minimal. For example, in discharging their responsibilities in the human rights area, UN secretaries-general have often been constrained by the UN Charter, especially Article 2 (7) which prohibits intervention "m matters which are essentially within the domestic jurisdiction of any state." This part of the Charter has previously been interpreted in a manner by which it has indirectly shielded dictators from international scrutiny of their human rights records. However, in his address to the General Assembly in September 1999, Kofi Annan said, "nothing in the Charter precludes a recognition that there are rights beyond borders." This line of rethinking should be stretched further. With the rapid changes brought about by globalization, what was "essentially" within the domestic jurisdiction of states in 1945 may not remain so in this millennium. Therefore, it is incumbent upon UN "managers" to reinterpret the Charter to reflect the new global realities. It would be a travesty if the UN Charter were to serve as a hindrance to the evolution of state sovereignty. The imperative is to reinterpret the Charter consistently.

THE CHANGING GLOBAL CONTEXT

What is Globalisation? Technology and Culture

In the late-1990s, no conference is complete without a panel on globalisation. There is much disagreement on the meaning and extent of this phenomenon, but there is surely a basic reality at work which cannot be ignored. This reality is globalisation as technology-driven fact: electronic communication, declining transport costs, more flexible forms of economic organisation, and the growing importance of mobile assets (like finance and knowledge) establish an increasingly uniform horizon of production possibilities across national borders, integrating markets around the world and internationalising decisions about jobs and investment. The consequences of this process in a world of unequal producers and consumers are well-known - spectacular rewards for those well-endowed with the conditions required to take advantage of these opportunities; increasing pressures on those less well-endowed to sell their labour, family life or environment cheaply in order to make a living; and rising inequality between these two groups, both within and between countries.

In 1998, the combined income of three billion people in the Third World was less than the collective assets of 358 multi-billionaires; Bill Gates' fortune (prior to the late-summer stock-market crash) was worth more than that of the poorest 40 per cent of the US population put together. (UNDP 1998). Rather than solid and stable blocs of 'North and South', NGOs in the 21st Century will confront a rapidly changing patchwork quilt of poverty and exclusion that requires new and genuinely international responses - notwithstanding the continued presence of a hard core of absolutely-poor people in South

Asia and Sub-Saharan Africa. As recent events have demonstrated, the "new rich" (like those in East and Southeast Asia), and those previously well-provided for in social protection (like the former-Soviet Union) can become the "new poor" on an epic scale within a matter of a year. Inequality, exclusion and the insecurity they breed look set to drive global politics for the next generation and beyond.

Underlying these trends is a more controversial process of "globalisation as culture": the homogenising of values and aspirations to Western norms of individualism and consumerism - what Hobsbawm (1994) sees as the real "cultural revolution" of our century. The media - recently transformed into a truly global institution controlled by a small number of multinational corporations - now plays a key role in these cultural processes. Some commentators dismiss such conclusions as superficial - capitalism has always adapted to the local context; others see culture as pivotal in the coming "clash of civilisations" as those who see themselves threatened or disempowered by cultural re-colonisation take refuge in ethnic or religious identity, often violently expressed.

The conflicts that this process generates are considered in Section 3. Despite these divergent interpretations, all agree that there is considerable room for manoeuvre in retaining the potential benefits of globalisation-as-fact, while addressing the potential costs of globalisation-as-culture. The real debate is not whether globalisation exists and will continue (it does and it will), but about how its costs and benefits are distributed, and on that question there is little that is pre-ordained by technology or impervious to politics. The issue for our conference is clear: what role do NGOs have in re-shaping the processes of an evolving global capitalism so that all can enjoy the fruits of economic progress without losing what gives equal meaning to their lives?

On this issue there is no consensus. Some NGOs advocate de-linking from the world economy in order to promote self-reliance and protect local cultures; others think this unrealistic and opt for various forms of constructive engagement; while the most optimistic embrace globalisation as a progressive social revolution in the making. We hope the conference will explore these positions and look at what NGOs are doing to advance each of them in practice. There are unlikely to be any universal answers here, especially since so much received wisdom has been abandoned in the post Cold-War retreat from grand theory and simplistic 'either/or' strategic choices. We are all experimenting, and learning as we go. This has important implications for the future of NGO advocacy which are taken up in Section Three.

Responses to Globalisation: the Role of Civil Society

Despite the diversity that characterises these debates, there remains a common thread that runs through all NGO positions: civil society can act as a countervailing force to the expanding influence of markets and the declining authority of states. Although workers have less power in integrated markets, consumers have more; and while the erosion of national sovereignty does leave some groups more vulnerable to the abuse of unaccountable power, it also opens up more possibilities for civic organisations to link with each-other across national boundaries in new structures of governance, especially as information technology makes it easier to move from traditional hierarchies to more flexible networks and alliances. The potential globalisation of governance and decision-making is explored in Section 2, though it is worth remembering that access to IT is also skewed toward those with more power and resources.

The true extent and potential of civil society is a controversial subject, especially at the global level. Some perceive a fundamental "power shift" as state-based authority recedes, while others question the ability of non-state groups to fill the resulting political vacuum. These doubts apply especially to development NGOs because of their dependence on foreign aid and their non-representative character. Nevertheless, an increasing number of NGOs are diversifying their funding sources and generating high levels of their own income from a mixture of commercial ventures, cost-recovery and local fund-raising, especially in South Asia and Latin America. In the process, they are sinking roots into their own societies and assuming more of the characteristics of a genuine civic actor, rather than a service delivery contractor. The rise of civil society in the South is uneven and in many areas slow, but it is happening, and this obviously has important implications for NGOs in the North and for the broader global civic alliances that are taking shape around the world. The Johns Hopkins Comparative Study of the "Third-Sector" found more than one million such organisations in India and 210,000 in Brazil (Salamon and Anheier 1997). These are exceptional cases, but even where the number and range of civil society organisations is smaller, individual agencies are developing a research and policy-lobbying capacity to rival those in the North, alongside their activities in service-delivery.

Whatever else globalisation may be doing, it has not

changed the fundamental reality of poverty of assets - the maldistribution of productive resources, skills and capacities that lies at the root of the problem. Integrated markets increase the importance of some of these assets (like knowledge and organisational strength), and decrease the significance of others (the fixed factors of production), but the imperative of re-distribution remains.

NGOs have a vital role in advocating for it, especially where fuzzy-minded "Third-Way" thinking makes all talk of re-distribution unpopular. Underlying these inequalities are the power structures that discriminate against certain groups of people. There is a danger that civil society will be seen as a new "magic bullet", now that politicians are disenchanted with both state planning and "free" markets, ignoring the fact that exclusion results from the interlocking structures of social, economic and political power in which civic associations are also implicated.

Most NGOs believe that human rights standards and other social values can be mainstreamed through these power structures in order to spread their benefits and reduce their costs - whether in markets, politics or social discrimination. In that sense, the over-arching role of NGOs is to "help revision the world as an ever-growing web of non-exploitative relationships" (Fowler 1997).

Translating these principles into practice at different levels of the world economy is difficult and complex, but the case for doing so is clear. Despite the disagreements and probable future fragmentation of NGOs in both North and South, all agree that there are increasing opportunities to work together across institutional boundaries in order to influence the forces that underpin poverty and discrimination, finding partnerships and synergies where few existed before, and moulding not just a strong civil society but a society that is just and civil in all that it does.

Civil Society Responses at the Local Level

Confronting globalisation begins and ends at the grassroots level, where NGOs are already developing a number of strategies to help poor people address the realities of their position in global markets and play a creative role in re-shaping economic forces. First, by improving the endowments of the poor so that they can compete more effectively and achieve a basic level of security, voice and equality of rights, without which economic "alternatives" are impossible.

This continues the traditional NGO role of developing skills, confidence, capacities and forms of association, and improving access to credit, services and economic opportunities - but underpinned by a more systematic attempt to link different levels and sectors of the economy. Second, NGOs can turn market forces to the advantage of poorer groups by reducing the benefits normally siphoned off by intermediaries - using, for example, joint marketing associations like those supported by NGOs in Latin America (Bebbington 1996) or attempts by NGOs in South Africa to work with community associations to help them negotiate better contracts with commercial hunting and tourism concerns.

Third, civic groups are exploring alternative modes of production and exchange which are less costly in social and environmental terms, build more "social capital" for use in market settings (qualities such as trust, co-operation, and honesty), support men and women to combine their market and non-market roles to better effect, and distribute profits with a social purpose.

These deeper changes are crucial in addressing the Achilles heel of most empowerment strategies: a failure to think through what happens when people with less power obtain more of it - a fairer society in which people distribute the costs and benefits of social and economic change more equitably, or more competition against the background of existing gender and other inequalities? This challenge - the regulation of all exclusionary systems of power - is one that most NGOs have tended to ignore, but it is the key to an agenda for transforming capitalism rather than "humanising" it.

Small-scale innovations may be viable at a larger scale if they can be shown to generate material advances sufficient to eradicate absolute poverty, thus building the long-term public and political support that more radical alternatives currently lack. We hope that the conference will explore this issue in detail. At the opposite extreme, NGOs continue their role as carers of last resort, operating safety-nets, and providing welfare to the casualties of globalisation, especially in countries where the transition from protected markets has been far too rapid (as in the Former Soviet Union).

From the Local to the Global

At the national level, grassroots innovations need support from pro-poor macro-economic and social policies. Although globalisation does erode state authority, the re-distributive and protective functions of states remain paramount. There is a tendency among some NGOs to focus on global advocacy to the exclusion of the national-level processes of state-society relations that underpin the ability of any country to pursue progressive goals in an integrated economy - the task of rebuilding government capacity to negotiate, monitor and regulate global regimes;

the importance of pro-poor alignments in civil society and between civil society, business and government; and the role of domestic civic groups in combating corruption, pressing for institutional accountability, and preserving a social consensus in favour of economic reform. Few NGOs have given enough thought to their roles in these areas, partly because of a lingering suspicion of states in any form, and partly because of the temptation to "leap-frog" the national arena and go direct to Washington or Brussels. In sustainable development terms, this is a serious mistake. At the global level, successful strategies must be connected to supportive actions in other parts of the international system. Globalisation means, not only that NGOs must engage more strategically with market forces on a much bigger scale than before, but do so in ways which link micro- to macro-forces together in a coherent way. Examples include: linking alternative production systems to international fair trade networks that give them some security in open markets; holding corporations to account against minimum social and environmental standards negotiated locally but monitored across global supply chains; and altering patterns of consumption in the "global North" in ways which do not disadvantage producers in the "global South."

With their international presence and connections, NGOs have a natural strength in this field, and in some areas a good start has been made, especially in helping to build a movement for more ethical consumption, investment and trading. NGOs have been key players in attempts to reform corporate accountability, test out multinational codes of conduct, re-shape consumer demand, and alter patterns of global trade. Inevitably, enthusiasm tends to run ahead of actual achievements - there are limits to the extent to which market economies can be reformed - but the principles involved have now been identified, and much is already known about how to operationalise them in practice. The conference provides an opportunity to take stock of what is happening with a greater degree of rigor.

In the same vein, NGOs are becoming more strategic in their lobbying of the International Financial Institutions, the monitoring of international commitments (like Social Watch), and the democratization of global economic and other regimes (like the World Trade Organization and the proposed Multilateral Agreement on Investment). Although there has been little concrete progress in opening these regimes to civil society participation, they are likely to be the centrepiece of the global system in the 21st century and demand a concerted response. The beginnings of such a response are sketched out below. The inadequacy of the IFIs has become an issue on which there is an unusual global consensus. Their focus on ensuring that public sector finances are not overextended has led them to neglect the regulation of private financial transactions. The consequences - financial panic and massive over-exposure - are fuelling a global recession that has already cost the world 10 million formal sector jobs.4 Talk by the G7 leaders about 'a new global financial architecture' has not hidden the fact that they have little idea what this might look like, or even how new solutions might be negotiated to a more democratic (sustainable) consensus. Are NGOs any better prepared? Critiques of the World Bank and the IMF have been an easy game; redesigning the international system will require more complex analysis and more subtle proposals than the sweeping campaigns of the past.

Bibliography

- Ahmed, Saifuddin : *NGO Perception of Poverty in Bangladesh : Myth and Reality*, Osder Pub, Kolkata, 2007.
- Ashish Chandra: *Human Rights Activism and Role of NGOs*, Rajat, Mumbai, 2000.
- Batra, G.S. : *Rural Development Management*, Deep & Deep, Delhi, 2000.
- Biju, M R : *Development Management Under Globalization*, Mittal, Mumbai, 2006.
- Chandra, Puran : *NGOs: Formation and Resource Mobilization*, Akansha, Delhi, 2007.
- Dharmarajan, Shivani : *NGO Development Initiative and Public PolicyKanishka Pub*, Delhi, 2008.
- Elangovan, R : *Performance and Marketing Practices of Khadi and Village Industries*, The Associated Pub, Delhi, 2008.
- Fisher, Julie : *Non-Governments : NGOs and the Political Development of the Third World*, Rawat, Allahabad, 2003.
- Goel, O.P. : *Role of NGOs in Development of Social System*, Isha Books, Kolkata, 2004.
- Goonatilake, Susantha : *Recolonisation : Foreign Funded NGOs in Sri Lanka*, Sage, Delhi, 2006.

- Jeff, S.L.: *Management Training Strategies for Developing Countries*, Boulder and London, Lynne Rienner Publishers, 1987.
- Kumar, R. : *Administration and Management of NGOs : Text and Case Studies*, Deep and Deep, Delhi, 2004.
- Mahajan, Sushil : *NGO Training and Management*, Manoj Books, Delhi, 2008.
- Malik, R P S : *Water Resources in India : Development Management and Strategies*, Oxford University Press, New York, 2007.
- Mishra, Kaushlendra : *Development of NGO's and Civil Society*, Navyug, Delhi, 2008.
- Panigrahi, Santosh Kumar : *Role of the NGOs in the Empowerment of the Disabled*, Radha Pub., Meerut, 2004.
- Pawar, S.N. : *NGOs and Development : The Indian Scenario*, Rawat, 2004.
- Pruthi, R.K. : *NGOs, Civil Society and Global Future*, Raj Pub, Mumbai, 2008.
- Riley, John M. : *Stakeholders in Rural Development : Critical Collaboration in State-NGO Partnerships*, Sage, Delhi, 2002.
- Singh, Ravishankar Kumar : *Role of NGOs in Socio-Economic Development*, Abhijeet, Meerut, 2003.
- Tej, B S : *NGO's Role in Development of Modern Society*, Omega Pub, Meerut, 2007.
- Tina Wallace: *Development NGOs and the Challenge of Change : New Roles and Relevance*, Rawat, 2003.

Index

□□□